Finding a Career That *Works* for You
A Step-by-Step Guide to
Choosing a Career and Finding a Job

Wilma R. Fellman, M.Ed.

Specialty Press, Inc.
300 N.W. 70th Ave. Suite 102
Plantation, Florida 33317

Specialty Press, Inc.
300 N.W. 70th Avenue, Suite 102
Plantation, Florida 33317
(954) 792-8100 • (800) 233-9273

Copy editing: Dara Kates Levan and Alice Ehrinpreis

Printed in the United States of America

ISBN 1-886941-38-6

Library of Congress Cataloging-in-Publication Data

Fellman, Wilma R., 1946-
        Finding a career that works for you / Wilma R. Fellman.
                p. cm.
        Includes bibliographical references and index.
        ISBN 1-886941-38-6
          1. Vocational guidance--United States. I. Title.

HF5382.5.U5 F466 2000
331.7'02'0973--dc21   99-087817

DEDICATION

This book is dedicated to my husband, Arnie, who has lovingly taught me the meaning of the phrase "team player." His encouragement has enabled me to fulfill a dream, beyond my expectations!

In loving memory of my parents, Betty and Henry Zaft, and my father-in-law, Dr. Abe C. Fellman, who taught me to keep reaching out for growth and dignity, never compromising one for the other.

TABLE OF CONTENTS

ACKNOWLEDGEMENTS

Finding A Career That Works For You could easily have remained a thought, an outline or a proposal had it not been for the support of several treasured people, including those mentioned below.

Ellyce Field, an accomplished writer and friend, who suggested that hitting a literary brick wall often requires backing up and starting over. Her graphic ideas for helping me track each chapter of this book saved it from the wastebasket at least three times!

Alice Ehrinpreis, my friend, editor, and sister-in-law, who offered her expertise at a moment's notice, tirelessly reading with amazing focus and correctness. I admire and appreciate her skill, as well as her gentle manner of transmitting the truths.

My mother-in-law, Betty Fellman, whom I adore, and who remains my role model for a woman of character, curiosity, intelligence, grace and dignity. I cherish and appreciate our relationship.

The daily cheers of Terry Matlen, Debbie Fellman, Jon Rose and Janice Cohen, who offered cyber encouragement in large, bold letters. The colored fonts were especially eye-catching and prompted me onward just "one more day."

My children, Rick Danuloff, Jeff Danuloff, Lainie and Peter Geary; grandson, Ryan Geary; sisters, Arline Bittker and Madelon Yarows; puppy, Murphy O. Fellman; and friends, who offer unconditional love and support for whatever project I leap into. They've all shared precious attention with this book for the past 2 years. I appreciate their patience.

Roberta Parker, for her help in naming this book. Sometimes when we go in circles, the most wonderful ideas come out over a pizza lunch!

I want to thank those career development experts who graciously agreed to be readers during the final stages of this book: Judith Hoppin, M.A, L.P.C, N.C.C.; Rhonda Brown, M.Ed., L.P.C., N.C.C.; Rosemary Doyle, M.Ed.; and Roberta A. Floyd, M.A., L.P.C., N.C.C. Their guidance, support, suggestions and encouragement helped to validate the quality of this resource. I appreciate the time and attention they took to give me feedback. I am thrilled that it so positive.

I am enormously grateful to my publisher, Harvey Parker, for his encouraging persistence and continuous pep talks. His insights, intuitive eye, and calm, professional determination directed this book into a product we can both be proud of. I've enjoyed our sparring and appreciate his willingness to listen to my pleas to include some "fluffy" wording that demonstrates how I would speak with a client.

Finally, I could never have completed this project without the cheerful support of my husband, Arnie Fellman, who has encouraged me every step of the way, despite hearing daily complaints about self-imposed torture. His loving reassurance has enabled me to share with others, far beyond my range of clients, who will hopefully benefit from this resource.

Wilma Fellman
February, 2000

INTRODUCTION

How do people decide what careers to choose? How can they know that what they choose will really be a good career fit for them? As a career counselor since 1983 I have met with hundreds of people who have felt lost—not seeing a clear career path in the future. Within a few short weeks, using a systematic method of career development skills, these individuals begin to show optimism and excitement at the options that lie before them.

You may be wondering what career direction to choose, or you may have a friend or loved one who is hoping to find the right career path. This book was written in an effort to lay out the steps necessary to learn career development skills, and thus find a career that works!

This is not a simple process. We are talking about directing very complex beings who have interests, accomplishments, skills, aptitudes, personality preferences, dreams, values, and a host of other ingredients that mix together to influence their career options. For some people there seem to be no options. For others the options may appear so great they are overwhelming.

How can one choose from a list of careers, knowing little to nothing about the day-to-day tasks and demands of each? Will the job chosen work for tomorrow as well as five or ten years down the road? Will the career you choose today still be needed in the future? Finally, will you find success in your career despite any barriers or disabilities you may have?

To help you choose the career path that may work best for you it is important first to develop the skills necessary to understand yourself better and to understand the different types of occupations that may be right for you. Part I of this book teaches important skills to help you become more aware of yourself and potential careers. Take the time to do the exercises in each chapter. While they may be as challenging as physical exercises, they also have the same big payoff! You will use the results of these exercises to help you in Part II of this book—finding a job. You will learn the skills necessary to write a winning resume and an eye-catching cover letter. You will be able to interview for a job better than your competitors. And you will learn important tips about starting a new job.

Throughout this book are examples of real people who love their jobs. These individuals are featured before each chapter, and have agreed to share with readers the idea that you can, and should strive to find a career that *works* for you.

If you are reading this for your child (even your adult child), spouse, friend or other loved one, tell this person that there is a systematic process that can take him or her to a knowledgeable position of good career decision making. Stress that this process is not instant. It takes time, but the time is well worth it in the overall picture. Encourage this person to do the exercises in each chapter and offer to provide valuable feedback for strengths you and others have seen in him or her. Point out that the job market is in constant change, and that things will look different each year. For this reason, learning the skills of career development can help your loved one this year, five years from now, or anytime in the future when there is a new crossroads.

If additional support is needed for special circumstances, contact organizations that represent that challenge, such as: CHADD (Children and Adults with Attention Deficit/ Hyperactivity Disorder), National ADDA (Attention Deficit Disorder Association), American Cancer Society, Cerebral Palsy Institute, Association of Learning Disabilities, American Heart Association, Council for the Blind and others that offer information and support for special needs. They often provide advocates to assist in learning about legal rights, accommodations, and other work-related information.

You can also encourage your loved one to "sample" some careers of possible interest. There is detailed information within this book about how to do that through internships, job shadowing, volunteering and temporary work that enables an individual to obtain firsthand information about what a job feels like within its environment.

Finally, you might want to suggest career counseling to help synthesize the materials gathered, sort out the options, help with proper decision making and provide ongoing support in planning a strong career path. In these and many other cases, career counseling can help ensure that the job chosen will work in the long run and can help erase vague, gnawing doubts.

It's hard to watch a loved one flounder. We'd like to fix all problems immediately and eliminate the pain. We can help by providing the skills necessary to make good choices, and then we must step back to watch the growth. Sometimes our loved one needs time to absorb all of this, in which case working at any job might be a way of taking the pressure off making a snap decision. Love and encouragement are always important ingredients for support while this process is underway.

Learning the skills of career development is a no-lose situation! Exercise your right to the best future you can find! You will find a career that *works* for you!

Part I

Learning About Yourself
and Your Future Career

PEOPLE WHO LOVE THEIR WORK

Name: Dennie Skidmore (Skid)

Hometown: Waterford, MI

Job title: Assembler--General Motors

Basic tasks of the job: Machine and assembly of all trailing axles for GM

What I enjoy about my work: I have 34 years with GM, and I enjoy this job because of the good wages and benefits that we receive as GM employees. I get satisfaction from taking pride in my work on the job, building a good quality product for a satisfied customer, who hopefully will continue to purchase GM vehicles. I enjoy the physical aspects of this job and knowing how to do all the jobs on the assembly line.

Advice for those thinking about this type of work: Have pride in yourself and be well trained in order to build a quality part for the vehicle. You must work together as a team and have communication between management and workers. If you work for any of the Big Three automakers, you will be rewarded with a pension and insurance for the rest of your life after retirement!

Chapter 1

UNDERSTANDING THE PROCESS OF CAREER DEVELOPMENT

Chapter Highlights

- Deciding upon a career that works for you can be an exciting process, but it takes time and skill.
- In the first step of this process you will better understand your interests, skills, values, work habits, and other personal traits, and how they match with different careers. You will finish part one of this book with a clearer sense of what careers interest you and what occupations you should consider within different fields.
- In the second step, you will focus on the job hunt itself—finding job opportunities in the career field you have chosen, preparing resumes and cover letters, and interviewing for jobs.

Lydia's Story

"I come from a small town where all the other students in my class seemed to know right from elementary school what they wanted to be 'when they grew up.' I never did. I am now 21 and about to finish college, but I still don't know what kind of a career I want! I'm starting to panic. I'm totally overwhelmed. What's wrong with me? Should I get a book on the hottest jobs for the future? I've heard that cyber jobs are the way to go. Should I sign up for a computer course to add to my training? What if I get all the way through that course and I discover I hate the jobs in that area?

I like animals; maybe I should get a job where I could care for them. I might really enjoy social work, but I'm told you can't make any money in that field. Would it be stupid to go into something where the salary is low? I'm running in circles. Help!"

How Do You Begin?

Lydia, 26 years old, went to school with friends who appeared highly focused, even at the elementary school level. Lydia was quiet as she listened to her friends chat about their career dreams. Lydia had no dreams. She had no clue about her vocational interests or career strengths. She was an unremarkable student, managing to get B's, with an occasional A or C. Lydia made up career goals just to feel she fit in with those around her. As she approached high school graduation, she began to feel desperate to find herself. Upon entering college, she chose a general major and felt her career decisions could be put off for a while. In her junior year she went to a career counselor to help sort things out.

Through the process of career counseling, Lydia became more aware of her vocational interests and aptitudes. She began to prioritize exactly the things she was looking for in a career. She became more confident of her skills and abilities as her counselor helped her recall many of her past accomplishments. She considered how her temperament and personality might lend themselves to certain careers and how they might not be suitable in others. She gradually felt more relaxed and was able to use the information she learned in career counseling to focus on different career paths.

After considering these factors, she decided to pursue a career as an accountant. She graduated from college and eventually became a certified public accountant. She worked at a small, easy-going firm. As a hobby, she participated in community theater and enjoyed a great deal of career and personal satisfaction.

Most People Don't Know What They Want

Some people seem to be born knowing what they want to do with their lives. We've all heard people make such statements as, "I just always knew I wanted to be a teacher" or "I've dreamed of being an automotive engineer." All of their thoughts about the future pointed in one direction. Education and training pursuits also supported the goal. It was a wrap!

But what if you are not one of these lucky people? You are certainly not the only person on earth who doesn't know what career direction your life should take! Most people don't clearly envision their future careers until they are mature adults. Others may never feel they have found themselves, even as they approach retirement.

If you are one of the many who aren't sure about your career, what should you do?
- Read a book about the hottest jobs for the future and select one?
- Find out what jobs are best for people who love animals? hate science? have learning challenges? are gifted students?
- Follow a path that you heard was good for people like you?
- Take that test—the one that tells you the path to take?
- Jump in and try out a career and just see how it goes?

None of these strategies is comprehensive enough. Instead, you should try a systematic approach to career decision making. Many people spend more time deciding what to wear than they do planning a career. Career counselors use a well-defined process to help people find suitable careers. We have included many of the steps in this process in this book. The purpose of these steps is to teach you two very specific sets of career-search skills that you could rely upon for years and use any time you are at a career crossroad.

Skill Set # 1: Learning About Yourself

The first set of career-search skills involves learning more about yourself. We have provided simple, yet informative checklists and inventories to help you become familiar with your interests, accomplishments, aptitudes, values, personality attributes, drive, work habits, and career dreams. These personal characteristics make you unique. Your career search is a very personal journey. Learning more about what interests you, how to identify your skills and aptitudes, your personality profile, and what motivates and energizes you will enable you to make career decisions that will be well suited to you in different areas. If you have any special challenges or disabilities you will learn about job accommodations and U.S. laws that protect against discrimination in the workplace.

Skill Set # 2: Hunting for Job Opportunities

The second set of career-search skills has to do with the actual job hunt—identifying trends in today's labor market, finding companies for which you might want to work, and presenting yourself to such companies. This involves learning about resources that can help you locate companies who need employees with the skills you possess. You will learn about using classified ads in newspapers and trade newsletters, the advantages and disadvantages of making direct contact with prospective employers, using the Internet to locate jobs, and using employment agencies and search firms to facilitate your job hunt. In this section you will learn the skills necessary to prepare resumes and cover letters and to present yourself in job interviews to make the best impression on prospective employers. The process doesn't end with obtaining a job. It is essential to learn how to avoid burnout and to evolve within your career to a lifetime of job satisfaction.

Nothing is etched in stone. As you learn, sometimes you change your mind and thus change your plan. That's perfectly all right. As you learn, sometimes you discover that you were almost "right on" but you need to modify your journey just a bit for maximum effectiveness. This may seem like a much longer way to go when it comes to choosing your life's work than simply dreaming up an option, but this is a guaranteed no-lose situation. In a world with so few guarantees these days, it's comforting to know that it is 100% guaranteed that you will always make a better choice with more information. The more you learn about yourself, the better your judgements will be.

Since life is a process and not a single performance, we must expect that one path may lead us to another that we did not expect. We can't be afraid of such changes, provided we've done our homework to determine that our careers will still work well for us.

You may want to learn about available support services that can help you get started, learn, grow, and evolve in your new career. Today there are reading materials, videos, counselors, therapists, coaches, and others that can help you. Just as a talented basketball player needs coaching to assure success, so do many career seekers. A supportive network of people often makes the difference between success and failure.

Don't Underestimate Your Success Potential

It is important that you read this book with an open mind about your future career and your potential to succeed. There are many myths associated with the career decision-making process. Believing in myths can limit your choices. Don't make the mistake of operating under false assumptions because of something you heard or something someone told you. Get to know your "work self" by going through the process you will read about in the chapters to follow. Let's consider some common myths that can lead you astray in choosing an appropriate career.

23 MYTHS ASSOCIATED WITH CHOOSING A CAREER
1. All people who are good in music make successful musicians.
2. All people who struggled in high school should avoid higher education.
3. All people interested in math should become mathematicians.
4. All people who learn differently (LD) should go to vocational training programs.

 5. All people with ADD are creative and should own businesses.
 6. All people with good grades become top professionals.
 7. All people who are blind should go into computer science.
 8. All people who were poor in math in high school should avoid math in college.
 9. All people talented in art can earn a living as fine artists.
10. All people who are good students become good employees.
11. All people who are good with people should go into sales.
12. All people with disabilities need to settle for their second or third choices or go on public assistance.
13. All people who dream of being actors should move to Hollywood or New York.
14. All people who have difficulties sitting still should avoid office jobs.
15. All people interested in brain surgery should go to medical school.
16. All people with ADD should avoid detail work such as accounting.
17. All people who make career changes later in life are discriminated against.
18. All people with good educational backgrounds do well in careers.
19. All people stick with their original career choices throughout their lives.
20. All people with special challenges can expect to achieve less in their lifetimes.
21. All people should choose careers that are predicted to be "hot" for the future.
22. All people who made career choice mistakes should start over.
23. All people have one true career destiny.

Dealing with Special Challenges

If you are an individual with a physical disability that affects your ability to see, hear, lift, move about, etc. or if you have an attention-deficit/hyperactivity disorder (ADHD) or a learning disability (LD), you may worry about whether the steps we have outlined in this book would work for you. They have for others with similar challenges, and we are confident that you can meet with the same success. Everyone has personal challenges of one sort or another that may interfere with job performance. Instead of tossing aside an otherwise great idea for a career because of the threat of challenges, work with someone who can help develop strategies, modifications, and accommodations that might make it a good match for you. Understanding your specific needs and communicating them to a prospective employer can often improve your chances for success. Specific information about ways to do this is provided.

Summary

There is a systematic process available to help you find a career that will work for you. This process involves learning different skills to help you understand yourself better, to understand changes in the current labor market, and to find a job and present yourself to prospective employees. Throughout this book, you will find many checklists and exercises to help you learn these skills. You will also be directed to resources in your community and on the Internet to help you identify and learn more about career fields that might be right for you. The career-search process will take some time and patience. By following the steps described in this book, you may end up with a career in which you can find success and satisfaction.

PEOPLE WHO LOVE THEIR WORK

Name: Mike Babel

Hometown: New York, NY

Job title: Actor, Director, Writer

Basic tasks of the job: Being totally real in unreal situations. Doing things vulnerably, publicly that most people would do behind closed doors. Having a willingness to fail every day. Constantly facing your fears and insecurities.

Why I enjoy my work: Because I discover myself, who I am, everyday, in everything I do.   I think I add to the available stock of reality in a positive, loving way and I keep my contribution to the Illusion to a minimum. My life is about being me. Everything I do provides me with the opportunity to find and live the greatest version of the grandest vision I ever had about myself.

Advice for those thinking about this type of work: Being an artist isn't something you choose, it's something you are. Get out of the way and let it unfold. Don't be afraid of it. It's not a job, it's your entire life. What you do IS who you are. It eventually, beautifully comes together. It's all self expression.

Chapter 2

UNDERSTANDING YOUR CAREER INTERESTS

Chapter Highlights

- Individuals who work in fields that interest them are more satisfied and productive in their jobs.
- Interests can be assessed through informal checklists and standardized tests. Fields that interest you can also be identified by examining the topics you like to read about, your hobbies, and how you spend your free time.
- After identifying fields that interest you, the next step is to find occupations or jobs within those fields for which you have skills (or for which you would like to receive training to learn necessary skills to perform the job).

Why Is It Important to Consider Your Interests when Choosing a Career?

Research has shown that individuals who work in fields of high interest to them are more satisfied and productive in their jobs than those who work in fields that do not interest them. Identifying fields that interest you will be the first step in finding a career that will work for you.

As mentioned earlier, some people are quite aware of career fields that interest them. They may have known from an early age that they wanted to go into a certain field. Others become interested in specific fields as they go through high school or college, or while working. Parents, teachers, friends, the media, and our personal tastes often combine to shape our fields of interest.

Within each of these fields there are many different occupations. For instance, you may be interested in filmmaking. You may have enjoyed watching movies as a child and still enjoy them just as much as an adult. When you look at the credits at the end of a movie you can get some idea of the variety of occupations that exist in the field of filmmaking (i.e., acting, directing, production, sound, visual effects, set design, costume design, casting, writing, marketing, etc.). The specific occupation or job you have in your chosen field may depend on the skills you have that enable you to perform the job competently.

Six Interest Clusters for Careers

In general, jobs fall into one of six interest clusters (or may be a blend of more than one).

1. Realistic (practical) jobs are "hands on." They usually result in some tangible product at the end of the task. Typical fields that fall into this category might be carpentry, prosthetics, repairing, outdoor work, or technology.

2. Investigative (probing) activities, such as analysis, inquiry, or research, require in-depth focus on one thing for a long period of time. Typical investigative fields are research, mathematics, and natural or medical science.

3. Artistic (creative) fields, such as drama, music, writing, art, commercial art, or graphic arts, involve self-expression.

4. Social (assisting) fields involve helping others, and require you to be interested in working in a service, teaching, or care-giving capacity. Examples might include social work, teaching, nursing, or physical therapy.

5. Enterprising (business) jobs are typically those that require some competitive edge to sell, manage, or persuade others. Some enterprising fields are corporate management, inside/outside sales, business start-up, product or service marketing or promotion.

6. Conventional (organizing) jobs work best for those who are detail oriented and capable of sticking with those details day to day. Some conventional jobs might involve accounting, organizing, data processing, office work, or record keeping.

Exercise 2.1

List the six interest clusters in order of "most like you" to "least like you."

1. _____
2. _____
3. _____
4. _____
5. _____
6. _____

Exercise 2.2

Check off the types of job activities that would interest you most.

___ working with my hands   ___ building things
___ fixing things   ___ solving problems
___ doing research   ___ being artistically creative
___ expressing myself   ___ teaching others
___ helping others   ___ selling products or services
___ managing others   ___ persuading others
___ making a lot of money   ___ promoting a product or service
___ doing office work   ___ keeping records
___ processing data   ___ organizing information
___ taking risks   ___ learning new things
___ being a leader   ___ making decisions
___ working at my own pace   ___ working with a team
___ competing with others   ___ growing plants, fruits, vegetables
___ working with animals   ___ working on a computer
___ writing stories   ___ writing ads
___ planning events   ___ making speeches
___ operating machinery   ___ writing creatively
___ writing technical material   ___ being outdoors
___ working regular hours   ___ selling merchandise
___ promoting a service   ___ changing activities often
___ traveling often   ___ raising money for charitable causes
___ competing with others   ___ speaking a foreign language

___ other_____

___ other_____

___ other_____

Exercise 2.3

Another way to identify fields that are of high interest to you is to examine the things you like to do in your leisure time. Take a few minutes to answer the following questions.

1. What types of books do you read for pleasure?

_____

_____

_____

2. Which magazines do you subscribe to or like to look through?

_____

_____

3. What activities do you do in your leisure time?

_____

_____

4. What subjects in school did you find most interesting?

_____

_____

_____

5. What are your hobbies?

_____

_____

_____

Exercise 2.4

The following list represents a sampling of occupations listed in the *Dictionary of Occupational Titles (DOT)*, published by the U.S. Department of Labor. The *DOT* is a valuable resource for first-time and experienced job seekers who want a comprehensive description of job duties. Over 27,000 occupations are included. Jobs that are similar are grouped together and are classified by a nine-digit code. The *DOT* covers nearly all jobs in the U.S. economy.

Read the list of occupations below and highlight the occupations that interest you. Don't worry if you don't really know what the occupation involves. After you have finished highlighting, choose 5 that appear most interesting and write them in the space provided at the end of the list. Later you can look these occupations up in the *DOT*.

DOT Code	Occupational Title	DOT Code	Occupational Title
001.061-010	Architect	001.061-018	Landscape architect
001.167-010	School-plant consultant	001.261-010	Drafter, architectural
001.261-014	Drafter, landscape	002.061-014	Aeronautical engineer
002.061-018	Aeronautical test engineer	002.061-030	Stress analyst
002.167-010	Value engineer	002.167-014	Field-service engineer
002.261-014	Research mechanic/Engineering technicians	003.061-010	Electrical engineer
003.061-030	Electronics engineer	003.061-046	Illuminating engineer
003.061-050	Planning engineer, central office facilities	003.161-014	Electronics technician
003.281-010	Electrical Drafter	005.061-014	Civil engineer
006.061-010	Ceramic design engineer	007.061-010	Automotive engineer
007.061-014	Mechanical engineer	007.061-026	Tool designer
007.167-014	Plant engineer	008.061-018	Chemical engineer
011.061-026	Welding engineer	012.167-054	Quality control engineer
017.281-034	Technical illustrator	193.167-014	Broadcast technicians
020.067-014	Mathematician	020.167-010	Actuary
022.061-010	Chemist	024.061-018	Geologist
030.162-010	Computer programmers	030.062-010	Computer scientist
040.061-014	Animal scientist	040.061-018	Dairy scientist
040.061-054	Soil conservationist	041.061-014	Animal breeder
041.061-030	Biologist	041.061-034	Biophysicist
041.061-054	Histopathologist	041.061-090	Zoologist
045.061-010	Psychologist, developmental	045.107-010	Counselor
045.107-022	Clinical psychologist	045.107-042	Vocational Rehab. counselor
050.067-014	Market-research analyst	070.101-018	Dermatologist
070.101-026	Family practitioner	070.101-066	Pediatrician
070.101-094	Surgeon	072.101-010	Dentist
072.101-014	Oral and maxillofacial surgeon	072.101-022	Orthodontist
073.101-010	Veterinarian	070.107-014	Psychiatrist
074.161-010	Pharmacist	075.264-010	Nurse Practitioner
076.107-010	Speech pathologist	076.121-010	Occupational therapist
076.121-014	Physical therapist	076.127-010	Art therapist
076.361-014	Respiratory therapist	076.364-010	Occupational therapy assistant
077.127-014	Dietitian, clinical	078.364-010	Ultrasound technician
079.101-010	Chiropractor	079.101-018	Optometrist
079.101-022	Podiatrist	079.167-014	Medical-record administrator
079.361-018	Dental assistant	079.362-010	Medical assistant
079.362-014	Medical record technician	079.364-026	Paramedic

17

079.374-022	Surgical technician	092.227-010	Teacher, elementary
094.227-030	Teacher, learning disabled	097.221-010	Instructor, flying
100.127-014	Librarian	100.167-030	Media specialist, school library
110.107-010	Lawyer	119.267-026	Paralegal
131.262-018	Reporter	131.267-026	Writer, technical publications
141.061-014	Fashion artist	141.061-018	Graphic designer
141.061-026	Illustrator, medical and scientific	141.061-034	Police artist
142.051-010	Display designer	142.051-014	Interior designer
142.061-026	Industrial designer	142.081-018	Package designer
143.457-010	Photographer	149.021-010	Art teacher
150.027-014	Drama teacher	150.047-010	Actor
151.027-010	Choreographer	160.162-018	Accountant
162.157-018	Buyer	162.157-038	Purchasing agent
165.167-014	Public-relations representative	166.267-014	Hospital insur. representative
166.267-026	Recruiter	168.267-010	Building inspector
168.267-014	Claim examiner	182.167-014	Landscape constractor
186.167-046	Property manager	186.267-018	Loan officer
193.162-018	Air-traffic-control specialist	195.107-034	Psychiatric social worker
195.107-038	School social worker	195.367-018	Community worker
196.263-010	Airplane pilot	199.167-014	Urban planner
199.281-010	Gemologist	201.362-010	Legal secretary
203.362-014	Credit reporting clerk	205.362-018	Hospital-admitting clerk
205.362-026	Customer service representative	209.687-014	Mail handler
210.382-014	Bookkeeper	214.387-010	Billing-control clerk
216.362-026	Mortgage-accounting clerk	219.482-010	Brokerage clerk
222.387-050	Shipping and receiving clerk	237.367-038	Receptionist
235.662-022	Telephone operator	238.367-018	Reservations agent
238.367-038	Hotel clerk	243.367-014	Post-office clerk
249.367-014	Career-guidance technician	250.257-010	Insurance sales agent
250.357-022	Sales representative	250.257-014	Financial planner
250.357-014	Residential leasing agent	254.357-014	Advertising sales representative
279.357-042	Burial needs salesperson	293.157-010	Fund raiser
295.467-026	Auto rental clerk	299.361-010	Dispensing optician
299.367-018	Watch/clock repair clerk	310.137-010	Restaurant host
313.361-014	Cook	313.381-010	Baker
316.681-010	Butcher	323.687-014	Housekeeping worker
330.371-010	Barber	331.674-010	Manicurist
332.271-010	Cosmetologist	332.271-018	Hair stylist
339.361-010	Mortuary beautician	339.371-010	Electrologist
352.367-010	Airplane flight-attendant	355.377-010	Occupational therapy aide
355.674-014	Nurse assistant	365.361-010	Luggage repairer
365.361-014	Shoe repairer	372.367-014	Jailer
372.563-010	Armored-car guard/driver	372.667-010	Airline security representative
372.667-018	Correction officer	373.364-010	Fire fighter
376.367-014	Detective	406.687-010	Landscape specialist
408.664-010	Tree trimmer	418.674-010	Dog groomer
446.161-010	Fish farmer	452.687-010	Forest worker
600.280-022	Machinist	601.260-010	Tool-and-die-maker
601.280-030	Moldmaker/die-casting/plastic molding	620.261-010	Auto mechanic
620.261-034	Auto cooling-system diagnostic technician	620.281-010	Air-conditioning mechanic
621.261-018	Flight engineer	621.281-014	Airframe/power plant mechanic
623.281-038	Motorboat mechanic	624.281-010	Farm equipment mechanic
637.261-034	Solar-energy system installer	638.281-018	Millwright
653.685-010	Book bindery worker	700.281-010	Jeweler
712.381-030	Orthodontic technician	712.381-042	Dental ceramist
716.280-018	Optician	716.382-010	Contact lens lathe operator

DOT Code	Occupational Title	DOT Code	Occupational Title
723.381-010	Electrical appliance repairer	730.281-014	Musical Instrument repairers
780.381-018	Furniture upholsterer	783.381-022	Luggage maker
804.281-010	Sheet-metal worker	807.261-010	Aircraft body repairer
810.382-010	Welder	821.261-010	Cable TV installer
824.261-010	Electrician	829.281-022	Sound technician
860.361-010	Boatbuilder	860.381-022	Carpenter
861.381-014	Bricklayer	862.361-010	Furnace installer
862.381-030	Plumber	864.381-010	Carpet layer
865.361-010	Mirror installer	866.381-010	Roofer
891.687-010	Chimney sweep	905.663-014	Truck driver, heavy
906.683-022	Truck driver, light	910.363-014	Locomotive engineer
970.281-018	Photograph retoucher	976.687-018	Photofinishing lab worker

The five occupations I highlighted that appear to interest me the most are:

DOT Code   Occupational Title

_____   _____

_____   _____

_____   _____

_____   _____

_____   _____

Finding Out About Jobs that Match Your Interests

If you find a job in the *DOT* that is of interest to you and you want more information about this job you can refer to the *Occupational Outlook Handbook (OOH)*. This is the U.S. Government's premier career reference book on occupations and future job markets. For over 50 years this volume has been used by career counselors, students, and other job seekers. It contains information on specific occupations. For each career, it describes work activities and environment, earnings, number of jobs and their locations, and types of education, training, and personal qualifications needed. The Bureau of Labor Statistics' projections of employment to the year 2006 are used to evaluate the kind of job opportunities that will probably be available for different occupations.

You can start your career search RIGHT NOW, by looking up some of the job titles that attract your attention the most. Be sure to allow your eyes to "wander" when you are looking up job titles in the *DOT* or the *OOH*, because you may find other options that are clustered around the specific one you are researching. This is the time to explore!

Standardized Interest Tests

Another way to identify your career interests is to take a standardized interest test. An interest inventory can be helpful in directing you toward a field; however, it will not give you all the information you need to make a career choice. Some examples of widely used interest inventories are:

- Campbell Interest and Skill Survey
- Career Assessment Inventory
- College Major Interest Inventory
- Kuder General Interest Survey
- Self-Directed Search
- Strong Interest Inventory

We cannot include any of the standardized interest inventories listed above in this book. Some places to go to obtain a thorough assessment of your vocational interests might be a school/college or university career center, career/vocational services center, private career counselor, or psychologist/social worker specializing in career issues.

What if Nothing Sparks Your Interest?

What if you can't identify any field that interests you? Not having a strong interest in any specific area can be the result of many things. The most common reason is that you may not have been exposed to many tasks, activities, jobs, careers, etc. This is often the case for students in high school or college who have not had much work experience. Without some work experience you would not have a strong frame of reference to make comparisons.

Feelings of discouragement can be another reason people sometimes have difficulty identifying fields that excite them. Sadness or low self-esteem can often result in having little or no interest in career fields. It may be helpful to see a career counselor or other health care professional if this is an obstacle for you.

If you didn't find any areas of high interest to you, here is what you can do:
1. Look through the Sunday "want ads." You may be able to get an idea of different types of jobs and a description of the skills required for them.
2. Go to the library and view various career-related videos to spark your interest.
3. Consider working as a temporary worker. This can give you first-hand experience about different work settings.
4. Volunteer to work for a charitable organization or other work setting that might be interesting to you.

Summary

Understanding your career interests and finding a job that matches these interests will improve your chances of being happy and successful in the career you select. Determining where you fit within six broad interest clusters and then learning about different occupations within these interest areas is a good way to start the career-search process. Resources published by the U.S. Government, such as the *Dictionary of Occupational Titles* and the *Occupational Outlook Handbook,* describe different U.S. occupations. These books, available in public libraries, college or university career centers, or at career counseling offices in your community, are a valuable resource. Understanding your interests and occupations that match them is the first step in your career search.

PEOPLE WHO LOVE THEIR WORK

Name: Magdalena Picco

Hometown: Pembroke Pines, FL

Job title: Head Cashier

Basic tasks of the job: Act as head cashier; check out (balance) cash drawers of all cashiers; make deposits (by computer); prepare cash/checks for daily Brinks deposit; order office supplies, cigarettes, and film; telephone bank daily to order change in several denominations; assist with Customer Service when they are short-handed.

Why I enjoy my work: I enjoy working with people. I enjoy being independent. I love my schedule, 6 am - 2 pm, because I am a morning person.

Advice for anyone thinking of doing that type of work: Learn as much as possible from wherever possible. Be polite and efficient. There is never "nothing to do," so you have to be the type of person who likes to keep busy.

Chapter 3

IDENTIFYING YOUR SKILLS AND ACCOMPLISHMENTS

Chapter Highlights

- Prospective employers look for job applicants who have the skills and experience necessary to perform the job well. Identifying your skills is an important part of the career-search process.
- Your accomplishments often reveal skills that can be useful in the workplace.
- Work skills fall into one of three categories—skills useful in working with information, with things, or with other people.
- People prefer to choose careers that match their work skills.
- Communicating skills to prospective employers in a resume, cover letter, and interview will be necessary when you are ready to hunt for a job.

Looking at Past Accomplishments

We all have some accomplishments that we can look back on with pride. Whether they are small or great, accomplishments tell us about the skills we possess that might be useful in the workplace. That is why it is important to identify accomplishments.

Identifying even small achievements can be helpful. Recollections of others' appraisals of your behavior can often lead to discovering special talents. Perhaps an art teacher commented on your unique style in high school pottery, or an English instructor encouraged you to enter an essay in a school contest. You might remember the sense of satisfaction at mastering a difficult computer application, completing a woodworking project, preparing delicious meals, sewing a dress, writing a paper, leading a work group, organizing an event, etc.

Tiny elements of excellence can be threaded together to tell a story about you. Similar threads in artistic, outgoing, leadership, performance, or verbal skills are seen from childhood and adolescence through mature adulthood. Although these threads can change, depending on what happens in your life, you may be able to pick out a pattern of strengths throughout your history of accomplishments.

This step will help you identify your accomplishments. It is important to start as early as your memory permits. You will probably recall many significant achievements; however, not all of them have relevance to your current career search. If you identify an accomplishment, does that mean that you should find a career associated with it? Would the art teacher's comment necessarily indicate that you should become a sculptor? No. It could be that your eye for art might lead to a position marketing art products or services.

Larry's Story

"I'm 50 years old, have a wife and two great, nearly grown kids. I haven't been happy in my career for many years, and I know it's taken a toll on my family, too. My mood has often been sullen, and I'm not much fun to be with! My greatest fear became a reality when the company I'd worked for more than 25 years underwent a massive 'streamlining.' My employers 'downsized' me right out of my position! I was devastated. I put my whole life into that job. I sacrificed many ball games with the kids to work overtime, and that's the reward I got.

"I don't know where to go from here. I began working at my company right out of college, so my resume is limited, as is my experience base. I'm not exactly at a desirable age to be looking for work now, and I'm not even sure I could stress my skills enough to make it through an interview."

Larry was depressed. His self-concept had been rocked by his "out-placement," and although his company was going to pay for counseling as a benefit of termination, he saw no rosy picture on which to build optimism.

Larry was asked to recall as many accomplishments as he could, beginning with his public school days and continuing to the present. His response to this assignment was quick: "That's the really sad thing. I really don't have any accomplishments and certainly not any that would impress a prospective employer." It was impossible to believe that a bright, 50-year-old man who had worked for 25 years, achieving middle-management status in a large, metropolitan corporation, was without accomplishment.

Larry's story is not unusual. During times of disappointment and discouragement it is easy to overlook your accomplishments. People often downplay their accomplishments or don't fully appreciate the abilities and skills they possess. It is important not only to fully appreciate your accomplishments, but to be able to tell prospective employers about them in resumes and interviews. Sometimes people have difficulty describing a skill or they may feel awkward boasting about skills they have. The exercises presented below will help you become aware of your past accomplishments and skills.

Exercise 3.1

Recalling Past Accomplishments

Complete the questions below to help you identify significant accomplishments.

1. What subjects in school were easiest for you?

_____   _____

_____   _____

2. What skills did you possess that enabled you to succeed in these subjects?

_____

_____

_____

_____

3. What strengths do you think your family/friends have seen in you?

_____

_____

_____

_____

4. What strengths do you think your teachers have seen in you?

_____

_____

_____

_____

5. What strengths do you think your employers or supervisors have seen in you?

_____

_____

_____

6. What adjectives best describe strengths in your personality (i.e., ambitious, friendly, perceptive, etc.)?

_____

_____

_____

7. What are at least five accomplishments you achieved in school, at work, or in community/volunteer activities?

_____

_____

_____

_____

8. What skills are required to accomplish such achievements?

_____

_____

_____

_____

_____

9. What things about your job performance set you apart from most people?

_____

_____

_____

10. Look over your responses to items 1-8 and list 3 to 5 of your greatest strengths below.

_____

_____

_____

_____

_____

If you find it too difficult to respond to a particular item, come back to it later. Ask a close friend or family member to provide feedback for your lists. Review previous school or job performance evaluations to spark your memory.

Accomplishments Help Identify Your Transferrable Skills

Our skills that might be useful in the workplace are transferrable skills. Richard Nelson Bolles, author of the best-selling book, *What Color is Your Parachute?*, regards transferrable skills as the basic building blocks of job performance. According to Bolles, transferrable skills can be divided into three groups: skills useful when working with data (mental skills), skills useful when working with people (interpersonal skills), and skills useful when working with things (physical skills). *Employers are primarily interested in knowing about your skills*. You will communicate them in your resume and interviews.

An important step in searching for a job is to identify, through your training and accomplishments, what your transferrable skills are. Transferrable skills cannot be determined by your job title alone. For example, an automobile mechanic may have a very broad range of skills (general repairs) or a narrow range of skills (transmission specialist). To accurately understand your transferrable skills you should answer the question "I am a person who can…"

Exercise 3.2

Look at the following list of skills. Which skills are your best? Check off all the skills that answer the question: "I am a person who can_____."

Mental Skills
I am a person who can:

___ research information	___ interview others	___ study
___ read	___ observe	___ copy
___ use a computer	___ work with numbers	___ analyze problems
___ organize things	___ prioritize	___ plan
___ file	___ gather information	___ present information
___ sort	___ transcribe	___ write
___ take notes	___ synthesize information	___ manage money
___ calculate	___ keep records	___ file
___ memorize	___ enable others to find things	

Interpersonal Skills
I am a person who can:

___ take instructions	___ help others	___ serve others
___ advise others	___ confront others	___ entertain others
___ influence others	___ teach others	___ communicate in writing
___ train others	___ supervise others	___ communicate orally
___ motivate others	___ counsel others	___ diagnose and heal
___ refer people to others	___ perform to a group	___ organize a group
___ entertain a group	___ lead a group	___ teach a group
___ plan events for a group	___ persuade a group	___ negotiate
___ assess people's strengths and weaknesses	___ motivate or sell to others	___ represent others, interpreting their ideas

___ communicate to groups by speaking or writing	___ communicate to groups by presenting	___ play an instrument, sing, act
___ guide discussions within a group	___ manage or run a business or event	___ follow through and get things done
___ initiate activity, new ideas	___ resolve conflict among others	

Physical Skills
I am a person who can:

___ work with my hands	___ use a keyboard	___ fix things
___ load things	___ move things	___ stack things
___ calibrate machinery	___ assemble things	___ disassemble things
___ carry	___ set up machinery	___ monitor operations
___ sew, weave, do crafts	___ cut, carve, chisel	___ paint, refinish, restore
___ fashion, model, sculpt	___ do precise work	___ build things
___ wash, clean, or prepare	___ train animals	___ take care of people
___ handle, expedite things	___ cook	___ manufacture, produce
___ do precise work with tools	___ repair things	___ set up machinery
___ operate or control machinery, vehicles	___ repair or maintain machinery, vehicles	___ construct rooms or buildings
___ model or remodel rooms or buildings	___ cause things such as plants to grow	___ take care of plants or animals

Example of an Ad That Describes Work Skills

To give you an idea of how skills can be described, review the ad below which was posted for the position "Divisional Manager for Community Affairs and Wellness" for a large national company. The following job skills were required:

- Communicating with others: Ability to effectively communicate with others, orally and in writing, and demonstrate effective listening skills.
- Speaking and presenting: Ability to speak clearly, concisely and persuasively with others in one-on-one or group settings.
- Persuading and influencing others: Ability to persuade others to accept a point of view and to influence the actions of others (e.g. getting others to commit to a specific program).
- Flexibility/adaptability: Ability to change or adapt work practices, priorities, procedures, or to change the scheduling of activities in response to fluctuating conditions or work demands.

- **Planning and organizing**: Ability to set priorities, plan, and coordinate work activities and obtain and manage resources so that work objectives are accomplished in a timely fashion.
- **Initiative**: Ability to think and take constructive actions at work on your own initiative. Skill and ability to take the lead in presenting and implementing new ideas or work methods.
- **Attention to detail**: Ability to work in an environment in which strict standards must be followed. Ability to be precise and accurate while paying close attention to detail.
- **Interpersonal Interaction**: Ability to develop and maintain positive working relationships with supervisors, co-workers, associates, and customers and handle conflict situations.
- **Professional behavior**: Ability to maintain composure and present a professional image when working with co-workers and customers.
- **Ethical behavior**: Ability to demonstrate responsible and honest behavior in all roles at work.
- **Leadership:** Ability to lead by example and demonstrate appropriate values. Ability to take initiative and show confidence when needed.

These represent only a small sample of work skills that employers may be seeking. Since the above example involves a position requiring a great deal of community and co-worker interaction, interpersonal skills are heavily emphasized. Positions that involve working with machinery or information would, of course, have totally different skill requirements.

Skill Words List

On the following page is a list of over 200 commonly used "action" words that may be used to describe skills. You can refer to this list when doing Exercise 3.3, which asks you to list five to ten of your skills. Refer back to the sample want ad for an example of how skills can be phrased.

Skill Word List

accessing	accommodating	accomplishing	accounting	achieving
acting	adapting	addressing	adhering	administering
advertising	advising	advocating	allowing	analyzing
anticipating	appointing	arbitrating	arranging	articulating
ascertaining	assembling	assessing	auditing	authorizing
automating	balancing	bargaining	bartering	booking
brainstorming	brokering	budgeting	building	buying
calculating	calling	capitalizing	caring	cataloging
charting	checking	cleaning	collecting	communicating
comparing	competing	compiling	completing	complying
conceptualizing	consolidating	contracting	converting	conveying
coordinating	corresponding	creating	debating	deciding
delivering	detailing	detecting	determining	designing
developing	directing	discovering	distributing	drawing
driving	editing	eliminating	empathizing	enabling
enforcing	establishing	estimating	evaluating	examining
explaining	expressing	filing	fixing	forcasting
formulating	gathering	generating	getting	guiding
handling	hanging	heading	healing	helping
identifying	illustrating	impressing	improving	improvising
increasing	influencing	informing	initiating	innovating
inspecting	integrating	inventorying	investigating	learning
listening	locating	logging	maintaining	making
managing	mastering	matching	measuring	mending
mentoring	monitoring	motivating	navigating	negotiating
noticing	opening	operating	observing	ordering
organizing	overseeing	painting	paying	predicting
preparing	problem solving	programming	promoting	presenting
proof-reading	providing	publicizing	publishing	questioning
raising	recalling	recruiting	reducing	refinishing
registering	rehabilitating	remembering	repairing	reporting
researching	restoring	saving	selling	serving
sewing	sharing	sharpening	shelving	showing
singing	sorting	starting	stopping	supervising
supplying	surveying	synthesizing	tabulating	teaching
testing	training	transcribing	traveling	treating
trouble-shooting	tutoring	typing	understanding	undertaking
unifying	uniting	upgrading	verbalizing	washing
weaving	weighing	welding	winning	word processing
working	writing			

Exercise 3.3

Now prioritize your skills by listing five or ten that are your best. If you have skills not included in the above list, write them down as well. Later you may use this list when preparing your resumes and cover letters to send to prospective employers.

1. _____

2. _____

3. _____

4. _____

5. _____

6. _____

7. _____

8. _____

9. _____

10. _____

Another way to identify your skills is to read through some careers in the *DOT* or *OOH*. Skills required for specific jobs are listed. After reading about several jobs, add the skills you have to the skills you have listed in Exercise 3.3. Review how you described your skills. You will use this list to describe yourself to prospective employers when you create your resume and prepare for the interview process, both of which will be discussed in Part II.

> Accomplishments: tiny elements of excellence
> threaded together to tell your stories.
> With the threads you can weave
> a richly textured tapestry
> that wraps around you
> declaring what makes you
> special.

Summary

People tend to search for careers in which they will be able to utilize skills they have acquired in the past, either through training or work experience. Identifying your skills and matching them with careers that use them is an important step in the career-search process. Employers want to fill positions with people who have the necessary skills to perform their jobs successfully. Communicating to employers, through resumes, cover letters, and in interviews, the skills you have identified in this chapter will be important in landing the job you want.

PEOPLE WHO LOVE THEIR WORK

Name: Scott Heemstra

Hometown: Columbiaville, MI

Job Title: Finish Carpenter

Basic tasks of the job: I do custom interior woodworking of all types.

Why I enjoy my work: I enjoy coming up with new ideas and being able to see my own finished product. It's very rewarding to get positive feedback on something that I did with my hands. I take pride in doing an excellent job.

Advice for those thinking about this type of work: Buy the best tools money can buy. When starting out, look for someone who does the best work in your area, and learn from them.

Chapter 4

IDENTIFYING YOUR PERSONALITY TYPE

Chapter Highlights

- Personality preferences affect your comfort zones in a job.
- Personality preferences can be measured and your type of personality can be identified.
- Results from personality assessments can help you make better career decisions.
- Personality assessments can help you improve your work habits, increase your career options, and enhance job performance.

What Are Personality Types and Why Are They Important to Consider When Choosing a Career?

As you know, people vary widely in their personalities. Are you the type of person who is quiet and feels more comfortable solving problems by yourself? Or do you prefer to develop ideas by talking with friends and co-workers?

Perhaps you are the type of person who notices everything. Your attention to detail with your five senses is excellent. You are systematic, organized and feel most comfortable when provided with clear, step-by-step instructions. On the other hand, you might be someone who misses the details, but is good at envisioning the overall picture.

Do you make most of your decisions with your head or your heart? If you had to fire someone, would you see that as a logical consequence of poor performance, or would you be too upset, thinking of how that person might feel hearing the news? Are you the type of person who prefers to collect facts and data before choosing a car, or do you buy one solely based on how much you like the appearance?

Are you more comfortable in situations that are highly structured, organized and predictable, or do those situations seem too rigid or boring to you? Do you do best with a list of things to do, or do you prefer to have your day just "unfold"? Is it important to you to plan everything in advance, or do you like last minute changes and deviations to a plan? Are you always on time, or is time management a challenge for you?

We could go on and on describing different personality types. In fact, experts in human behavior have developed many personality models to explain differences in people's behavior, preferences, and styles of interacting with others and with their environment.

When making career decisions it is important to consider how your personality preferences fit with the requirements of the work you will be doing and the job setting. If you are the type of person who prefers working with things rather than dealing with people, you may want to steer clear of careers that require a great deal of social interaction. If you are a highly energetic, competitive, and adventuresome person who enjoys challenges, change, and variety in your day, you may become bored and frustrated with an office-based job that is too routine and structured.

Personality types are defined in terms of innate preferences we have for doing things a certain way. When we gravitate towards work environments that mesh with our personality types, we generally find more comfort and job satisfaction. We are naturally drawn towards things that allow us to be more on automatic, and we are drawn away from things that are awkward for us. Consider for a moment how it would feel if you could not use your dominant hand for writing, eating, throwing a ball, etc. You can learn to do more with your non-dominant hand, but it would feel awkward and would require more focus and attention. You might tire more easily and certainly tasks that seemed simple before would take you much longer to complete. Similarly, if your personality type doesn't mesh with your job requirements or work setting, you may feel quite awkward and out of place. Understanding how important your personality type is can bring you one step closer to finding a career that works for you.

Melinda's Story

Melinda worked for a telemarketing division of a large communications company. She was required to make hundreds of calls a day to identify potential leads who would want to subscribe to a new telephone service plan. Melinda took her responsibilities seriously. Each day she set out to meet her quota of telemarketing calls. She was not the persuasive type and had a rather quiet disposition. She could not easily sell the benefits of the new service, even though she had a sales script to follow. It took so much energy out of her just to muster the enthusiasm required to sound convincing that she was totally burned out at the end of each day. She wanted to be alone in the evenings to replenish herself for the next day. This was not a good job match. Melinda eventually left this job and found another sales position that didn't require an instant "hard sell." She felt more relaxed and found herself so energized by the end of the day that she was able to take up some new hobbies. This career match worked for Melinda, as it nurtured her personality type instead of draining it.

Mark's Story

"Sometimes I feel like a fake! I struggle in my supervisory duties, having difficulty giving negative criticism to my subordinates, even when it is needed. I'd rather do something over myself than hurt someone's feelings. I waited a long time for this promotion, but I am so uncomfortable. Every night I drag myself home and dread starting all over again the next day."

Mark had worked his way up in the company, from sales associate to manager. He had loved his job in sales and delighted in surpassing all sales quotas. For this reason, he was promoted to sales manager. Mark was so flattered that it never occurred to him to question the degree of match with the potential change in jobs. Mark found that management required a personality type that he did not possess. While he loved working alone, striving for his own goals, he found it difficult to direct the work of others. He was able to do all of the tasks of his new position, but detested the feeling he had each time he had to correct an employee. Mark decided to seek a job in which he could be responsible for his own work. He once again enjoyed the day-to-day tasks required, and he gained quick recognition as a high-powered sales representative.

Taking a Personality Inventory

Psychologists have developed a number of personality inventories designed to measure an individual's personality preferences. Because there are many different theories of personality, there are many different personality tests available. The tests most frequently used to understand personality type as it relates to career planning include the following:
- California Psychological Inventory
- Myers-Briggs Type Indicator
- Occupational Stress Inventory

- Personality Research Form
- Sixteen PF Personal Career Development Profile

The assessments listed above are all standardized tests. They have been rigorously developed and the test taker's responses are compared to others who have taken the test to provide the most meaningful results. As with the interest inventory discussed earlier, a personality assessment might be administered at a school, college, or university career center, at a career or vocational services center, or by private career counselor or psychologist, social worker, or other mental health professional specializing in career issues.

Exercise 4.1

Evaluate Yourself on Personality Factors

As previously stressed throughout this book, many factors go into creating a good match between you and your career. To speak of personality factors is to talk about dozens of preferences for taking on life in a way that is most comfortable. When you put these preferences together, the result is an understanding of your complex personality type. There are no simple checklists that do justice to this intricate patterning, yet it is important for you to see how your preferences can impact on your job choice.

Following are various scenarios that demonstrate some of the differences in personality type. While some may apply to you sometimes, decide which scenarios are most like you, most of the time.

Scenario A—External type
1. You prefer to interact with people
2. You "process" problems with others
3. You find interruptions a blessing
4. You prefer working with a group
5. You think out loud
6. You are thought of as talkative

Scenario B—Internal type
1. You prefer to read and think
2. You "process" on your own
3. You are annoyed by interruptions
4. You prefer working on tasks alone
5. You think first...then speak
6. You are quiet while others lead

If you are more like the type described in Scenario A, you might enjoy careers that allow you to be external—to work alongside others most of the time. Working as part of a creative advertising team, or as a fundraiser, real estate broker, team teacher or other group worker might be a good career fit for you.

If you are more like the type described in Scenario B (like Melinda described above), you might enjoy careers that allow you to be more internal or reflective, with time to think and process your thoughts before interacting with others. While you might still be very people oriented, you might enjoy solitary jobs, allowing your people energies to be used outside of work. Examples of these jobs might be accountant, engineer, editor, computer programmer, administrative assistant, or technical writer.

Scenario C—Detail type
1. You notice details
2. You need concrete evidence
3. You like following a step process
4. You seldom make errors

Scenario D—Overview type
1. You might miss details
2. You see by "instinct"
3. You might jump ahead
4. You often make errors

If you are more like the type found in Scenario C, you might be a more detail-type person who notices things you see, hear, smell, etc. All of these details come through our senses and imprint on our memories. Teachers, law enforcement workers, artists, dental hygienists and case management specialists all benefit from being this type of person.

If you believe you are more like Scenario D, you might be less comfortable having to notice details, but more comfortable as the overview type or idea person. You may have excellent instincts that would benefit you in such careers as therapist, consultant, musician, massage therapist, or creative writer.

Scenario E—Decisions by head type
1. You decide things using facts
2. You can work amidst tension
3. You might hurt people's feelings
4. You can tactfully direct others

Scenario F—Decisions by heart type
1. You decide things using feeling
2. You need harmony at work
3. You try to please others
4. You'd rather do it yourself

If you are more like the type described in Scenario E, you might find yourself able to take on roles that require you to "just go with the facts." You make your decisions using your head and concrete reasoning. You might be especially suitable for leadership roles, finding little problem directing others in either pleasant or unpleasant tasks. Career examples that might be suitable for you include: business management, human resources, private investigation, mechanics, or criminal law.

If you are more like the type described in Scenario F, you make most of your decisions with your heart. You'd resemble the story of Mark, above, who found it difficult to deal with directing others in unpleasant situations. He was extremely sensitive to the feelings of others, to the extent that it interfered with what he needed to do. If this sounds like you, your strengths might lie more in the areas of personal achievement, working in environments that are pleasant, value driven and independent. Career examples suitable for you might include social work, flower arranging, library science, religion or education.

Scenario G—Structured type
1. You manage time well
2. You hate schedule changes
3. You prefer a predictable life
4. You strive for closure
5. You prefer things organized

Scenario H—Unstructured type
1. You manage time poorly
2. You welcome surprised changes
3. You prefer a flexible life
4. You like keeping a project going
5. You prefer things laid back

If you believe you are more like Scenario G, you probably enjoy work environments that are structured. You like to know the rules and regulations and will stick to them. You are time oriented and seldom late. You most likely enjoy completing tasks rather than working on them over a long period of time. Adapting to change is a challenge for you and you do best when repetition is part of the work setting. You may be comfortable in a career as a medical records technician, air-conditioning mechanic, librarian, surgical technician or optometrist.

However, if you believe you are more like Scenario H, you probably enjoy "going with the flow," as an unstructured type. You might hate time, clocks and watches and would be more comfortable in a work environment where things go at a flexible pace. You enjoy working in a "multi-tasking" environment which allows you to start one thing and then set it aside while you work on another. You may be seen by others as disorganized, but you may have a sense of organization all your own. Examples of jobs in which you may be comfortable are creative art director, fashion artist, graphic designer, writer or photographer.

These sample scenarios demonstrate that there are differences in how people prefer to take on the world. These innate preferences need to be identified and put to best advantage when deciding on a career. If an internal person finds himself in an external career role, the struggle to keep up the "che charade" might only last so long before burnout occurs. If an overview-type person tries to keep up in a detail environment, the struggle threatens to deplete the worker's energy. If a heart decider needs to fire workers for the "good of the company," he might find himself physically sickened by the tasks ahead. If an unstructured individual is expected to function as a highly structured person, he might try modifications, accommodations, and strategies that lessen the struggle. However, he probably will never be comfortable working day after day, trying to push the "square peg into the round hole."

The goal is to identify your personality type and understand how it manifests on a job. Then you will be in a better position to make good career choices that nurture instead of deplete you. To fully accomplish this, consider having a personality assessment done with a career specialist. This type of guidance can help you interpret the results and use the strengths of your personality type to your advantage.

Summary

Understanding your personality type may give you some clues to the type of work environments in which you will function best. The scenarios described above will start you thinking about all the little personality differences that make you comfortable, like writing with your dominant hand. Learning whether you are external or internal, a detail type or overview type, a head decider or heart decider and structured type or unstructured type can help you make better choices. A career that works for you would be one in which most of the tasks of the job feel as though you are "writing with your dominant hand." As you read about careers in your research, listen for situations that you believe would nurture and energize you, as opposed to situations that might cause you endless struggle or burnout. If you would like to learn more about your personality type as it relates to work environments, you might consider undergoing a thorough personality assessment with a career development professional.

PEOPLE WHO LOVE THEIR WORK

Name: Gail L. Faulkner

Hometown: Southfield, MI

Job title: Vocational Rehabilitation Consultant

Basic tasks of the job: Provides leadership in areas of deafness rehabilitation, transition services to youth with disabilities, and mental health programming. Develops community-based services to clients with disabilities, businesses and others to reach a goal of employment for persons with disabilities.

What I enjoy about my work: The variety of projects, people interaction, working in teams, meeting new people and learning something new every day.

Advice for those thinking about this type of work: Have a great passion and care for assisting people in reaching life goals. Have excellent listening skills, enjoy working with people, be flexible, and be able to do many tasks or projects simultaneously.

Having said this, I am planning for a new career in the area of interior design. This has been a life-long dream, as I want to help others enhance their environment to greater comfort levels. I decided to make my hobby a reality.

Chapter 5

PRIORITIZING YOUR WORK AND LEISURE VALUES

Chapter Highlights

- People value different things in their work. It is useful to identify the things you would like to derive from work.
- Leisure values are also important to identify. You may be able to find a job that matches some of your leisure values.
- Values should be prioritized from most to least important so you can evaluate whether a job will really provide what you want.
- Careers that match your values (give you what you want) are the most rewarding in the long run.

What Are Values and Why Are They Important?

We value things about our jobs and our personal lives that are important to us and that allow us to have the things we want and be the type of people we want to be. Examining what is important to us, both in our jobs and elsewhere in our lives, is important when choosing a career. People are often most satisfied in careers that give them what they want, either directly or indirectly, as a result of their jobs.

Obviously, people vary a great deal in what they want from their jobs. Some people value financial security most. Others find helping others to be most gratifying. Some people find that the opportunity to be creative is the most important aspect of their jobs. They treasure the chance to work in an environment where they are encouraged to develop their ideas.

You may be the type of person who values a supervisory position, or you may prefer working for a large company over a small business. You may like variety in your daily activities, or you may value sameness and routine. You may enjoy working with animals or you may prefer working with people. If security is important to you, you may want a job that provides health and retirement benefit plans. If you find risk exciting, you may value jobs that offer less security but greater opportunity to succeed by your own actions. Before you go on your job search, you should have some idea of what things are important to you in your work. That is the focus of this chapter.

Irene's Story

"Five months ago my husband announced he wanted a divorce. I have been at home with the kids for the last 17 years and haven't even thought about working. Needless to say, my world turned upside down and I haven't been able to think clearly until now. I used to be a nurse, but feel totally out of the loop in terms of the current medical profession. If I went back to nursing, I'd probably have to take courses to brush up on my skills and become more marketable. I want a career that will support me and my children. I want a job that will challenge me yet allow me to perform competently. It is important that I have free time to spend with my family. I want health care and retirement benefits. I need to be home by the time the kids are out of school. I'll do anything that allows me to make the money we'll need. Whatever I do, I hope it's more fun and less demanding than my previous jobs. I hope it's creative, with less pressure. I guess I just really want it all!"

Irene's story reflects the challenge of finding a job that fits her values. As the 38-year-old mother of three sons, ages 17, 10, and 7, she values a job that will be challenging, will allow her to be home with her children, has less pressure than her previous job, allows her to be creative, and provides sufficient income and health benefits. She also indicates that she needs to work as soon as possible, as things are already starting to topple around her financially. Irene may severely limit her job options if she only considers a job that supplies her with all of the things listed above. She must prioritize what is most important to her and her family before going on her job search.

Value Assessments

Career counselors use a number of questionnaires and checklists to help people identify the things they value in a career. Below are several value assessment instruments. As with the interest inventories and personality assessment instruments reviewed earlier, these value assessment instruments can be obtained at a career counseling center at most colleges and universities or at local career counseling offices or agencies.

- Career Values Card Sort Kit
- Minnesota Satisfaction Questionnaire
- Values Scale
- Minnesota Importance Questionnaire
- Salience Inventory

Exercise 5.1

Work Values Checklist

Complete the Work Values Checklist below to identify elements of work that are important to you.

	Very Important	Moderately Important	Not Very Important	Moderately Important	Very Important	
work alone	___	___	___	___	___	work with others
work for organization	___	___	___	___	___	self-employment
well defined duties	___	___	___	___	___	plenty of room for creativity
be my own boss	___	___	___	___	___	work under someone else
help others	___	___	___	___	___	work with things or data
close supervision	___	___	___	___	___	little or no supervision
low level responsibility	___	___	___	___	___	high level responsibility
no critical decisions	___	___	___	___	___	make key decisions
35-40 hour work week	___	___	___	___	___	40+ hour work week/weekends
guaranteed regular hrs.	___	___	___	___	___	flexible hours
fix things	___	___	___	___	___	care for others
stay close to home	___	___	___	___	___	travel
variety of duties daily	___	___	___	___	___	similar duties daily
challenges and risks	___	___	___	___	___	security and safety
fast pace and pressure	___	___	___	___	___	slow pace and low pressure
visible end product	___	___	___	___	___	results of work not visible
short-term goal	___	___	___	___	___	long-range goal
work indoors	___	___	___	___	___	work outdoors
work to benefits others	___	___	___	___	___	work with little benefit to others
high dress requirements	___	___	___	___	___	low dress requirements
willing to relocate	___	___	___	___	___	work in specific geographic area
work for large business	___	___	___	___	___	work for small business
live close to work	___	___	___	___	___	live 1/2 hour or more away from work
work with machine	___	___	___	___	___	little work with machines
early retirement	___	___	___	___	___	opportunities after age 65
frequent travel	___	___	___	___	___	little or no travel
retirement savings	___	___	___	___	___	no retirement savings
contribute to society	___	___	___	___	___	no benefit to society
focus on personal goals	___	___	___	___	___	no focus on personal goals
weak earning potential	___	___	___	___	___	strong earning potential
poor health benefits	___	___	___	___	___	excellent health benefits
work with those in need	___	___	___	___	___	work with general population

Other values:

_____

_____

_____

Now look over your responses to this checklist. Copy the values that are in the Very Important columns in the spaces below. Later, when you are making key decisions about your career, you will use this list to be sure that whatever you are considering matches your top values.

Things I most value in a job:

1. _____

2. _____

3. _____

4. _____

5. _____

6. _____

7. _____

8. _____

Considering Leisure Values

Career counselors urge us to consider things in our lives that are important to us outside of work. These are called leisure values. Leisure values could include hobbies, interests, volunteer work, etc. For example, Kate has been home with her children for several years. She has had a strong interest in environmental issues. She is now looking for work and is considering a job with an environmental advocacy organization.

Matthew loves children. Having come from a large family he has always valued being around children. He might want to consider teaching, child care, pediatric health care or other occupations that would incorporate this value.

Tina believes in the wellness concept. She has adopted a rigorous exercise routine and values the time spent on working out and eating properly. Because she values these things so much she is considering a career as a health trainer, dietician, health educator, or health equipment sales representative.

Exercise 5.2

List three things that are important to you in your leisure time. These leisure values might give you some clues to finding a career that would be a perfect match for you.

Things I most value in my leisure time:

1._____

2._____

3._____

4._____

5._____

Summary

People often want different things from their jobs. As a result of working through the exercises in this chapter we hope you have a clear understanding of the things you expect your job to provide. It is useful to understand what you are looking for in a job and to prioritize how important these things are. It is difficult to find a job that provides you with everything you want, but if you go into your career search with a clear idea of what you would like, you have a better chance of getting the things most important to you.

PEOPLE WHO LOVE THEIR WORK

Name: Suzanne Halperin

Hometown: Chicago, IL

Job title: Director of Catering

Basic tasks of the job: Booking special events, planning and executing them, giving a party for Elton John and the cast of his new Broadway musical.

Why I enjoy my work: I enjoy constant action, meeting new and interesting people and working with a very diverse array of peers. The hospitality business is extremely hands-on and very interactive.

Advice for those thinking about this type of work: You must begin at an entry level position and prove yourself. This industry offers much growth potential as it has many different departments within a hotel. You must be very flexible with your schedule and it requires a demanding amount of hours. You must be the kind of person who can handle doing many tasks at once and keeping calm while under pressure.

Chapter 6

UNDERSTANDING YOUR APTITUDE

Chapter Highlights

1. Your aptitudes are important to consider when choosing a career. Identifying your aptitudes will enable you to increase your chances of success in school or on a job.
2. Aptitudes can be assessed through formal aptitude tests.
3. Aptitude in an area could lead to successful achievement.

What Are Aptitudes and Why Are They Important?

An aptitude can be defined as the ability to acquire proficiency in a specific area. An aptitude enables a person to perform well in a specific area. Aptitudes are often seen as innate, natural capacities to do certain tasks. However, aptitudes are not necessarily always inherited. They can also be learned.

Keep in mind that aptitudes are not skills. A skill is the ability you currently possess. An aptitude is your potential to acquire a skill based upon your natural talents or training. Since you are most likely to succeed at things that come easy to you, recognizing your aptitude will help you in your career search.

The requirements of any specific occupation may vary from one work environment to another and may call for different aptitudes. For example, the automobile mechanic who services cars will benefit from having good mechanical aptitude when it comes to diagnosing problems and fixing them. The automobile mechanic who manages the front desk at a repair shop may need excellent social aptitude to maintain good relations with customers. A musician who is part of an orchestra is required to play music and would therefore rely heavily on artistic aptitude, whereas a musician who teaches music needs to be able to instruct students as well and would need good social skills as well as artistic skills.

Marge's Story

Marge dreamed throughout her childhood of being a doctor. As a youngster she would play with her dolls and pretend to take care of the sick. Marge's excellent scholastic achievement in high school along with aptitude tests scores indicating strengths in the biological sciences encouraged her to select a pre-med major when she attended college. She eventually finished college and medical school and went on to become an emergency room physician.

Aptitude Tests Predict the Ability to Perform on the Job

Career counselors often use aptitude tests to better understand their clients' strengths. There are tests that measure single aptitudes such as manual dexterity, clerical skills, artistic ability, etc. Other aptitude tests are broad ranging and measure multiple aptitudes. For example, academic aptitude tests may measure the entire array of skills needed to meet the demands of an academic curriculum. Mechanical aptitude tests reflect all the skills needed to do mechanical work. Aptitude test scores are used to predict future performance in educational and vocational endeavors. The probability of performing well on a job, in a training program, or in college can be predicted pretty accurately by aptitude test performance.

Aptitude Tests in Use Today

Some of the most reliable, widely used aptitude tests include the following:
1. ACT Career Planning Program
2. Apticom
3. Armed Services Vocational Aptitude Battery Career Exploration Program (ASVAB)
4. Differential Aptitude Tests (DAT)   (also with Career Interest Inventory -CII)
5. Guilford-Zimmerman Aptitude Survey
6. Occupational Aptitude Survey and Interest Schedule-2 (OASIS)
7. General Aptitude Test Battery (GATB)

Exercise 6.1

The Differential Aptitude Test (DAT) is commonly used. Although we cannot include the DAT in this book, we have summarized the eight aptitude areas covered on the test for you to review. Following each are some sample jobs associated with that aptitude. Check off the areas in which you believe you have above-average aptitude.

_____ Verbal Reasoning. This is the ability to hear elements of a problem and think through to an answer or conclusion. Examples of careers that require good verbal reasoning are teaching, social work, sales, advertising, acting, medicine, and psychology.

_____ Numerical Ability. This is the ability to use arithmetic calculation and reasoning to solve problems. Examples of careers that require good numerical ability are accounting, bookkeeping, physics, design, architecture, banking, financial planning, and statistics.

_____ Abstract Reasoning. This is the ability to understand situations, objects and relationships that are not concrete. Examples of careers that require good abstract reasoning are engineering, industrial design, systems analysis, economics, operations research analysis, and urban planning.

_____ Clerical Speed and Accuracy. This is the ability to quickly complete clerical tasks, perform with dexterity on a keyboard, or succeed with other clerical technology. Jobs that require good clerical speed and accuracy are administrative assistant, executive secretary, court reporter, and record keeper.

_____ Mechanical Reasoning. This is the ability to understand how things work. Careers that require good mechanical reasoning are electrical work, plumbing, machine designing, robotics, transportation, and maintenance.

_____ Spatial Aptitude. This is the ability to visualize an image in your mind and move that image as needed. Careers that require good spatial aptitude are architecture, drafting, design, programming, and interior decorating.

_____ Spelling. This is the ability to have a good sense of sound formation and language construction. Careers that require good spelling aptitude are writing, teaching, editing, and administration.

_____ Language Usage. This is the ability to utilize good word usage, sentence structure, and paragraph formation. Careers that require good language aptitude are writing, teaching, editing, speaking, politics, and publishing.

Summary

We usually do well in the things in which we are interested, and we usually are interested in the things we do well. Therefore, identifying your areas of highest aptitude can help direct you to some career clusters you might not have previously considered. Once you've identified areas of aptitude you feel are your best, it is helpful to look at descriptions of occupations in the *DOT* or the *OOH*. This will enable you to compare your perceived aptitudes with the skills necessary for specific careers. Keep in mind that since aptitudes are innate as well as learned, it is always possible to improve upon an aptitude.

PEOPLE WHO LOVE THEIR WORK

Name: Ellyce Field

Hometown: West Bloomfield, MI

Job title: Freelance newspaper writer and radio contributor, author of family tour books

Basic tasks of the job: I write weekly parenting and family entertainment columns and calendars for *The Detroit News*, contribute a weekly family entertainment segment to WJR AM-760, and am the author of the *Detroit Kids Catalog* series, a tour book for Michigan families published every two years by the Wayne State University Press.

Why I enjoy my work: I have been able to work out of my home office for the last 16 years, while raising my three sons. It's allowed me the flexibility of working my deadlines and assignments around their school, vacation and extra curricular activities.

Advice for those thinking about this type of work: Working at home takes intense motivation, discipline and organization, plus an ability to self promote.

Chapter 7

RECALLING YOUR EARLY CAREER DREAMS

Chapter Highlights

- Your early career dreams may be a clue to the career you might want to pursue.
- You can look for jobs that relate to activities you may have enjoyed as a child or may have fantasized about while growing up.

Early Career Dreams

Some of the things we enjoyed as children influence the careers we seek as adults. For example, read what the following people remembered about the things they enjoyed doing in early childhood:

"In kindergarten I was chosen to be in the class play. I still remember how energized I felt in front of an audience full of people. I just knew that I was comfortable in front of a crowd. Now I'm a school teacher and the classroom is my stage. I love to present lessons to children and programs to parents and co-workers. It is funny how my early childhood experiences carried a clue to my future career.

"I used to dream about being a shopkeeper. I would set up my bedroom as a store, carefully arranging 'merchandise' all over my bed and dresser. I remember taking pride in how the store looked just before it was time to open. Then I would imagine people coming in to shop. It would always be pleasant. I loved pretending to meet people as they came to my store all day. As an adult I have found a wonderful career in sales. I enjoy seeing a variety of people each day and setting things up for 'show time.'"

"As a teenager I would work my problems out on paper. After an argument I would rush to my room to write like crazy until I had purged my feelings onto the written page. I dreamed about being a reporter or a novelist so that I could put my passion for writing to work. Today I work as a technical writer for an engineering firm and enjoy the tasks associated with writing."

Getting In Touch With Your Early Career Dreams

Some people knew from early childhood the careers they wanted to pursue as adults. Others never had a clue. Where do these early childhood visions come from? They often are the result of our early experiences—people we have met, stories we have read or which were told to us, television shows, movies, etc. For many people these childhood visions fade with time; for others they remain vibrant for years.

Exercise 7.1

Try to recall what you pictured yourself doing when you were younger. In what direction did you dream you might go?

As a child I wanted to be:

_____

_____

_____

_____

_____

_____

Exercise 7.2

Dream/Daydream Checklist

Check off any of the following if they have ever been one of your early career visions. Feel free to add some that may not appear. What do you think these say about you?

___	Astronaut	___	Veterinarian
___	Nurse	___	Actor
___	Teacher	___	Skater
___	Firefighter	___	Professional sports player
___	Singer/Songwriter	___	Inventor
___	Rock star	___	Researcher
___	Dancer	___	Writer
___	Cartoonist	___	Parent
___	Lion tamer	___	Race car driver
___	Circus clown	___	Opera singer
___	Police person	___	Truck driver
___	Sales person	___	Musician
___	Zoo keeper	___	Lawyer
___	Librarian	___	Scientist
___	Cattle rancher	___	Singer
___	Doctor	___	_____
___	Lawyer	___	_____

What do your choices say about you today?

_____

_____

_____

_____

Summary

The occupations you envisioned for yourself as a youngster might offer additional clues to career directions. Of course, dreams alone are not predictors of the path you should take in choosing a career, but they may provide some clues to some long nurtured areas of interest. Many people find jobs in careers they dreamed about as young children. They held onto these dreams and turned them into fulfilling realities.

PEOPLE WHO LOVE THEIR WORK

Name: Dave Fellman

Hometown Naperville, IL

Job title: Corporate Sales, Technical Support

Basic tasks of the job: I provide technical support for a group of outbound corporate sales representatives working for a $1.5B international company that sells computers and all related accessories and supplies. My job entails locating products that our customers are looking for, using telephone and internet search skills. I also provide technical training for newly hired sales reps, as well as ongoing training on new products.

Why I enjoy my work: It is hard to get into a rut; it is stimulating; and I don't have to "take my work home with me."

Advice for those thinking about this type of work: Attitude, attitude, attitude. Have a positive attitude about yourself and your company. Always have a smile on your face. Make decisions as though you were the president of the company. Be a team player. Be honest with yourself and with your co-workers. If you don't like what you are doing, change jobs.

Chapter 8

CONSIDERING YOUR
ENERGY PATTERNS

Chapter Highlights

- Some jobs require highly energetic people while others do not.
- Knowing your energy level and patterns may be helpful in your career search.
- Energy patterns can be identified by keeping a log.

Why Is Your Energy Pattern Important to Consider in Your Career Search?

Studies have shown that high energy, or stamina, is a characteristic that many employers are looking for in the people they hire. Some jobs require a highly energetic person who is able to work for long hours at a rapid or concentrated pace. Other jobs may not be as energy demanding. In such jobs workers may be able to plod along slowly and steadily. If you are a sprinter in a plodder's job you may become bored and restless. By the same token, if you are a plodder in a sprinter's job you may become fatigued, overwhelmed, and frustrated. Knowing your energy pattern can help direct you towards a job that matches your production flow. Consider the cases of Fred and Sue.

Fred's Story

"I wake up every day in a total fog. I am useless for the first hour of the day. Then, as the day wears on, I find that I begin to pick up steam and I can focus on tasks that seemed more complicated in the morning. I work in the medical records department of a major hospital, so I need to be accurate and focused. When I realized I work best in the latter part of the day, I began volunteering for the later shift at the hospital."

Sue's Story

"I was sinking in my job as an advertising executive. It seemed to require me to be 'on' from morning to night. It was too stressful. Once I analyzed my energy pattern I noted that it didn't match what was required for my type of job. I was more of a 'sprinter' locked in a 'plodder's' role. Now I work for a different firm that has a more laid back atmosphere. I'm so much more comfortable, as well as more effective on my job."

Logging and Identifying Your Energy Pattern

Identifying your energy pattern is simple. On a planner or calendar, write a number from 1 to 10 three times each day (at the start, midpoint, and end of the day). One means you have zero energy and 10 means you are highly energized. It's important to try to jot down the numbers at approximately the same time each day. Doing this for a couple of weeks is good. If you can track your energy patterns each day for a month, that would be even better. Usually a month is enough to get the information needed, but sometimes another month is required. If there is no pattern, that, too, is important information. It would suggest you might not need to watch for energy surges and slopes in order to do things well.

Summary

The amount of energy we bring to the workplace to fulfill job responsibilities can be a major factor in job performance. High energy people prefer to keep active, either mentally or physically, and enjoy the pace of a busy schedule. They thrive on stimulation and activity. People who have low energy levels tend to prefer sedentary, routine jobs that do not require bursts of energetic output and productivity. Understanding your energy patterns, when you are most productive, and what types of work environments best suit these patterns is important in your career search. Mismatches can often lead to worker or employer dissatisfaction.

PEOPLE WHO LOVE THEIR WORK

Name: Steven Halperin

Hometown: Jefferson, NJ

Job title: Marina owner/water ski instructor/snow
ski instructor (in winter)

Basic tasks of the job: In the summer, I take care
of the dock, help people with their boats, give water
ski lessons, and take camp kids on the super tubes.
In the fall, I winterize boats and store them. In the
winter, I do marketing for the next season. And in
the spring, I work on the dock. I do power washing,
put in plantings, put out chairs and tables for the guests, and get the property ready
for the next summer season.

Why I enjoy my work: I enjoy being on the water and being with people. I also
enjoy multi-tasks, movement, and risk taking.

Advice for those thinking about this type of work: Save your money to buy the
marina. Mine is small, but it's a good income. My job is great for people who
want to be their own boss, but it takes hard work during the summer months.

Chapter 9

UNDERSTANDING YOUR WORK HABITS

Chapter Highlights
- Besides skills, job success depends on attitude, dependability, sense of responsibility, commitment, and many other personal characteristics.
- Evaluating your strengths and weaknesses in these important areas can help you avoid poor job performance.
- Identifying work habit strengths can be helpful in preparing a winning resume and in performing well in an interview.

What Do Employers Want in an Employee?

When employers interview job candidates they look for people who have good skills. However, they also consider a positive and productive attitude and good work habits to be important. This chapter contains two exercises designed to help you become aware of how you rate in terms of these characteristcs. It might be helpful to complete these questionnaires yourself. You may want to ask someone who is familiar with you to rate you as well. You can use the information from these exercises in Part II of this book where you will be asked to prepare a job resume, cover letter, and interview information.

Exercise 9.1

Below is a list of 15 qualities that employers are generally looking for in the people they hire. After each one, give yourself a score from 1 to 4. This will show where you need to improve in order to be considered a highly valued worker.

	Not At All Like Me	Somewhat Like Me	Pretty Much Like Me	Very Much Like Me
1. Good communication	0	1	2	3
2. Positive Attitude	0	1	2	3
3. Flexible and adaptable	0	1	2	3
4. Try for above average performance	0	1	2	3
5. Good work ethic	0	1	2	3
6. Accepts responsibility	0	1	2	3
7. Productive, both quality and quantity	0	1	2	3
8. Honest and reliable	0	1	2	3
9. Willingness to keep on learning	0	1	2	3
10. Ability to solve problems	0	1	2	3
11. Good common sense	0	1	2	3
12. Creative	0	1	2	3
13. Intelligent	0	1	2	3
14. Well educated	0	1	2	3
15. High energy/stamina	0	1	2	3
16. Accurate	0	1	2	3
17. Attentive to details	0	1	2	3
18. Punctual	0	1	2	3
19. Good attendance	0	1	2	3
20. Work well with others	0	1	2	3

Fill in the statements below:

Based on the above ratings, my work area strengths are:

_____

_____

_____

Based on the above ratings, my work area weaknesses are:

_____

_____

_____

Exercise 9.2

Workplace Behavior Checklist

Employers need to hire the best candidate possible. Identifying your work habits can help you present yourself in your resume and interview in a positive way. For each workplace behavior, assess yourself on a scale of 1-5.

Rating Scale: Weak 1 2 3 4 5 Strong

Thoroughness
1.____ I plan well ahead when beginning projects.
2.____ I'm able to stick with detail-oriented tasks for long periods of time.
3.____ I think things through carefully before I speak or act.
4.____ My work is consistently high quality.

Memory
5.____ I'm able to remember details over time.
6.____ I'm capable of learning new material without taking notes.
7.____ Even when I'm rushed, I can still remember important items to consider.

Time Management
8.____ I use a calendar to schedule.
9.____ I plan large projects by breaking them down into smaller parts.
10.____ My desk/work area is neat and non-cluttered.
11.____ I'm able to make order out of chaos.

Communication
12.____ I get along well with co-workers.
13.____ I get along well with superiors.
14.____ I get along well with subordinates.
15.____ I can get my point across in conversations.
16.____ I'm able to express myself well in written communications.
17.____ I have proven to be a leader.
18.____ I enjoy working with others in group situations.
19.____ Previous employers would give me a good recommendation.

Paperwork
20.____ I'm able to coordinate paperwork.
21.____ I'm careful not to make mistakes.
22.____ I tend to take paperwork in stride and not get overwhelmed.

Rating Scale: Weak 1   2   3   4   5 Strong

23.____ I plan paperwork to be turned in on time.
24.____ My paperwork is orderly and neat.

Cognitive Strengths
25.____ I catch on quickly to new material and methods.
26.____ I read material easily.
27.____ Math is a strength.
28.____ I spell well.
29.____ I have a good sense of direction.
30.____ I am able to learn by whatever method I'm taught.
31.____ I love to learn new things.

Flexibility
32.____ I'm able to work various hours.
33.____ I'm able to work long hours without losing quality.
34.____ I'm able to work with noises, lights, air temperature, and other distractions.
35.____ I'm able to concentrate without quiet.
36.____ I can shift my focus as needed on the job.
37.____ I welcome changes.

Interpersonal skills
38.____ I'm well liked.
39.____ I consider myself a problem solver, not a problem creator.
40.____ I enjoy meeting new people.
41.____ People come to me for guidance.
42.____ My temperament is even each day.
43.____ I try to make others feel important and "heard."
44.____ I pride myself in getting along with difficult people.
45.____ I believe that a good employee makes it "work out," no matter what comes up.
46.____ I'm considered a positive person.

Fill in the statements below:
Based on the above ratings, my work area strengths are:

_____

_____

_____

Based on the above ratings, my work area weaknesses are:

_____

_____

_____

Summary

Employers are always looking for the best candidate possible. Skills are important, as are a host of other qualities that make an employee a pleasure to have around. Identifying your weaknesses will give you concrete ideas for improvement. Being able to discuss your strengths adds power to your resume and interview process.

PEOPLE WHO LOVE THEIR WORK

Name: Joy Ziraldo

Hometown: Ann Arbor, MI

Job title: Graphic Designer

Basic tasks of the job: I work for a mortgage company so the basics tasks are providing most of the materials the bankers send out. I design direct mail, postcards, print ads, and most of the internal materials as well. I also have done freelance work including logo development and corporate identities.

Why I enjoy my work: When people ask me what I do, I usually reply, "I make the world pretty." I enjoy my job because it allows me to be creative all day long. The project is different with each customer. Interaction is also a big part of it. I enjoy helping people put their ideas into a paper. Everyone has ideas. It's my job to help them develop them and make them look good.

Advice for those thinking about this type of work: I believe it was Confucius who said, "Choose a job you love and you will never have to work a day in your life." And I couldn't agree more. I have loved art ever since I can remember…and I turned this love into a career…it doesn't get any better than that. All work is hard…but not all of it is fun! In the field of graphic design there are plenty of options and opportunities. Grab them and be creative.

Chapter 10

COMPLETING
A JOB HISTORY

Chapter Highlights

- Preparing a job history is often necessary when developing resumes or completing employment applications.
- Besides being a chronological report of your past employment, a job history can include what you liked and disliked about past jobs. This information could be useful in choosing a future job.

What Is a Job History?

A job history is a chronological summary of the different jobs you have had. Maintaining an up-to-date job history is useful when completing resumes or employment applications. However, a job history is also important to document the different aspects of a job you liked or disliked.

All too often people go from one job to another looking for the perfect fit. Some people continually find themselves in positions in which they feel mismatched. Eventually they become unhappy with their jobs and look for ones that better match their interests, values, personality type, or abilities. Completing a job history forces you to keep track of the pluses and minuses of past jobs so you can make a better decision in the future.

Carol's Story

"It seems I've hopped from one mismatched job to another. Each time I've left a job I've headed for the next with the thought that, at the least, I wasn't going to be in the same awful situation anymore. But I found that the new situation only contained less of one distateful thing, and more of another! I often traded one unpleasant situation for another one."

Carol's resume appeared spotty. She had a series of jobs lasting from six months to two years. One would suspect, looking at the succession of different positions, that she was incapable of keeping a job for a long period. She reported that at the start of each job she thought she had found the perfect place for herself. Then, around six months into it she would begin to find problems and would want to move on to find "the right" job. If Carol had completed a job history she would have benefitted from having looked back at work patterns.

Exercise 9.1

Completing a Job History
List your jobs, beginning with the most recent.

Date of Employment	Name and Address of Employer	Your Job Title
_____	_____	_____
	_____	
	_____	

What you liked about this job.

_____
_____
_____

What you disliked about this job.

_____
_____
_____

Date of Employment	Name and Address of Employer	Your Job Title
_____	_____	_____
	_____	
	_____	

What you liked about this job.

_____

_____

_____

What you disliked about this job.

_____

_____

_____

Date of Employment	Name and Address of Employer	Your Job Title
_____	_____	_____
	_____	
	_____	

What you liked about this job.

_____

_____

_____

What you disliked about this job.

_____

_____

_____

Summary

Keeping good records of your jobs will be useful when preparing your resume and in recounting your work experiences during interviews. In addition, thinking about the enjoyable aspects of previous jobs will help you refine your search. Sometimes in job searches people tend to follow a pattern of mistakes as they rush to take a job that is similar to one they have had before in which they were unhappy. It is helpful to understand the parts of a job you like and dislike and to try to avoid work that emphasizes those things you dislike. Learn about yourself from your past. You will make better choices in the future.

PEOPLE WHO LOVE THEIR WORK

Name: Robert S. Sher

Hometown: Southfield, MI

Job title: Retired Chief Financial Officer, Coach and Volunteer

Basic tasks of the job: Helping people live a more efficient, stress-free life.

Why I enjoy my work: I only deal with people who are positive and want to grow.

Advice for those thinking about this type of work: It is very gratifying mentoring people and watching them try to achieve their full potential.

Chapter 11

SPECIAL CHALLENGES

Chapter Highlights

- Don't define yourself by your challenges or disabilities.
- In career development, start with your strengths and end with your disabilities or challenges.
- Be aware of protective laws in the workplace.
- Understand which reasonable accommodations can help you do your job.
- Decide how much to share with employers about your challenges.
- Test out a job to see if it works for you.

Carl's Story

Carl, 23 years old, was born without arms and one leg due to the horrors of a drug called Thalidomide. He was first seen in career counseling following nearly a year of fruitless attempts at employment. He had been raised by very strong parents who taught him that he had no disabilities, only challenges to overcome. He had a prosthetic leg that enabled him to walk. He drove his own car with an adaptive device that allowed dexterity with his "nubs," as he called them, which were elbow-length appendages from the shoulders. With these "nubs" he was able to hold a pen or pencil and control it to the extent that his penmanship was excellent! Carl was extremely bright, graduating Phi Beta Kappa from a major university with a degree in fine arts. His major was photography, and he hoped one day to be a professional photographer. In fact, he had won awards for his photographic work while at the university and was encouraged by his professors to continue in the field. Carl's career goal was to get a "day job" that would somehow be related to photography but would give him the steady income he needed to support himself while pursuing his great love. He had sold pieces of his photographic work, but needed a steadier cash flow. For these reasons, Carl had been applying to businesses that provided film processing.

Because Carl had been so strongly raised to concentrate on his strengths instead of weaknesses, he did not wish to discuss any disabilities with prospective employers. Instead, he walked into an interview and did not mention the obvious question in the minds of the interviewers: "How do you think you can do this job, as I see you have no arms!" In one year's time no employers had asked this potentially rude question and Carl had not wanted to discuss it. The outcome was that the uncomfortable prospective employer would quickly end the interview and not call Carl back for further discussion. Carl was proud and extremely frustrated!

Carl's career counselor decided that it would be in Carl's best interest to present him to a prospective employer. The counselor contacted an employer, who owned a fast film development company, explained Carl's challenges, and offered him a deal. If Carl could come to work for him for a week with no pay, would he try him out? Immediately the employer shied away from such a proposition because of the emotional concerns. If he didn't work out, how could he look Carl in the eyes and tell him he couldn't use him? It would be too difficult. The counselor finally agreed to be the one to break the news to Carl. Carl would work for one week, Monday through Friday. On Friday Carl would leave and simply say to the employer, "Have a nice weekend." Then the employer would call the career counselor and discuss how the week had gone.

On Wednesday of that week, the career counselor received a call from the employer. He stated that he had no idea how Carl was able to accomplish what he did, but he was the best he had seen at this kind of work! His performance was flawless as he carefully used his "nubs" to center the photographic materials in the floating chemicals! His speed was more than competitive with the other employees and he appeared at ease with the process. The employer indicated that he wished to hire Carl on Wednesday and pay him for that whole week. Carl was hired! Follow-up six months later proved that the "match" between Carl and his job was still good and that it provided him with everything he needed to concentrate on pursuing his dreams as a photographer.

Carl's story is a very important one. If a person with no arms and one leg can become a high-speed production worker in a technically skilled field, what limitations should people with other obstacles such as attention-deficit/hyperactivity disorder, learning disabilities, or other physical, emotional or mental challenges put on themselves?

Evaluating Career Options When Faced with Special Challenges

If you have a disability it may be important to identify your functional limitations in a way that employers can understand. For example, telling an employer you have diabetes does not help provide a "work around" solution or accommodation for you. However, telling an employer that because of your diabetes you have special requirements involving eating (you need to eat or snack more frequently than others to keep your blood sugar regulated) gives the employer a better idea of how to accommodate you.

Exercise 10.1

Below is a list of terms to help describe to an employer different types of functional limitations.*

balancing	hearing, total loss	seeing, total loss
carrying	judgment	speech, partial loss
climbing	learning	speech, total loss
communicating	lifting	stair climbing
concentrating	memory, long term	stamina
crawling	memory, short term	standing
fainting	operating foot pedal	stooping
feeling	paying attention	task sequencing
fingering	perception	thinking
grasping	planning	upper extrmeties mobility
handling	pulling	walking
hearing, partial loss	seeing, partial loss	writing

From: Witt, M. A. (1992). *Job Strategies for People with Disabilities*. Princeton, NJ: Peterson's Guides.

Only functional limitations that affect essential duties of the job you are seeking need to be considered by the employer when arranging for job accommodations. People who have injuries or who are disabled can often perform essential job duties once they have been accommodated. Employers can tailor work to meet the needs of an individual with a disability. The process begins with identifying functional limitations and extends to removing or minimizing workplace barriers that prevent an otherwise qualified person with a disability from achieving the expected outcomes of the job.

If you disclose your disability to your employer, it is your responsibility to let your employer know what accommodations you will need. Employers must make "reasonable" accommodations based upon the company's size and resources. You can get help with determining appropriate accommodations by contacting the Job Accommodations Network (JAN) at 800-526-7234. JAN, a service of the President's Commission on the Employment of People with Disabilities, is charged with providing accommodation information at no cost to businesses, rehabilitation professionals, and people with disabilities within the United States. This information is used to make appropriate accommodations in the workplace. JAN received nearly 80,000 calls from July 1994 to June 1995, the majority of which were from private or public employers of people with disabilities.

Most accommodations for people with disabilities are inexpensive and not as difficult to put into place as one might imagine. According to a 1994 report from JAN most job accommodations cost under $500 and many cost nothing at all. For example:

Problem: An employee who is confined to a wheelchair cannot use a keyboard because the desk is not high enough.
Solution: Raise the desk with blocks.
Cost: $0

Problem: An office worker with a back injury cannot bend down to retrieve reams of paper to load into the copy machine and printer.
Solution: Rearrange how paper is organized and stack reams on higher shelves in the storeroom.
Cost: $0

Problem: An employee with a writing problem cannot take notes during morning staff meetings.
Solution: Notes taken by another staff member are copied and given to the employee.
Cost: $0

JAN reports that within 90 days after calling, 38 percent of the employers who contacted them implemented an accommodation based on the information they were provided. Of those, 82 percent said that the accommodation was either moderately effective or very effective.

Some common accommodations made to help disabled individuals with functional limitations include: ramp stairs, wider doorways, accessible restrooms, wheelchair lifts, hand railings on stairs; hours adjusted to reduce commuting problems, rest periods with make-up time at the start or end of the work day, word processors, less frequent travel, handheld magnifiers, voice-activated dictation equipment, talking calculator, reorganized files or shelves, lowered or raised desks, support service assistants, changed job locations.

People with Attention-Deficit/Hyperactivity Disorder (ADHD) and Learning Disabilities (LD)

ADHD and LD may affect as much as 15 to 20 percent of our work force. These are neurological disorders that can seriously affect an individual's ability to perform at work. People with ADHD often struggle with problems related to distractibility, disorganization, poor memory, impulsiveness, and short attention span. They may get bored easily, lose their focus of concentration, and rush to get things done. They are prone to making mistakes. They can have problems with time management and completing extensive paper work. They can also have difficulty setting limits and may talk excessively. People with LD may have trouble with reading, written language, and mathematical computation. They may have difficulty comprehending instructions. They often exhibit problems with memory and recall and may have trouble organizing their work, meeting deadlines, and solving problems. ADHD and LD are invisible handicaps. They are not immediately obvious to others in the work environment.

Sample Work Adaptations for People with ADHD or LD
1. Meet with your supervisor more frequently for feedback.
2. Have clear guidelines written for job performance.
3. Ask your employer to reduce distractions in your work environment.
4. Request training in time management skills.
5. Use headphones to reduce distractions.
6. Do work in smaller chunks instead of long-term projects.
7. Use checklists to determine job priorities and set deadline dates.
8. Ask for clerical help with paperwork.
9. Use post-it notes as reminders of work that is to be done.
10. Ask for a private office when you need to really concentrate on a task.
11. Ask for help taking notes.
12. Use a word processor if handwriting is a problem.
13. Have a calculator available for mathematical problem solving.

It is important to remember that taking the time to find a career that works for you can cut down on the need for some accommodations. Trying to mash a square peg into a round hole is fruitless. Finding a job that fits well may require only minor adaptations that often need not be told to the employer.

The Americans with Disabilities Act (ADA)

Today there are laws that help to protect the individual with disabilities. The Americans with Disabilities Act (ADA) prevents discrimination in employment based strictly on disability. *Succeeding in the Workplace*, a book edited by Peter Latham, JD, and Patricia Latham, JD, outlines how the law works.

The Americans with Disabilities Act (ADA) outlaws discrimination against individuals with disabilities in private sector employment, state and local government employment, state and local government activities and programs, and public accommodations. In order to obtain protection, it is necessary to establish that you:

1. are an individual with a disability and have a physical or mental impairment that substantially limits one or more major life activities;
2. are "otherwise qualified" though possessed of a disability; you are eligible for the job, education, or program benefit with or without a reasonable accommodation;
3. were denied a job, education, or other benefit "solely by reason" of the disability.

The law applies to the employers in question. Attempts to enforce this law must be interpreted as "reasonable." If the employer is large enough to be covered by the ADA, then many accommodations will likely be considered "reasonable."

Reasonable accommodations include:

1. those required to ensure equal opportunity in the job application process;
2. those that enable the individual with a disability to perform the essential features of a job;
3. those that enable individuals with disabilities to enjoy the same benefits and privileges as those available to individuals without disabilities.

Examples of reasonable accommodations might include:

*   providing or modifying equipment or devices
*   restructuring the job
*   creating part-time or modified work schedules
*   reassigning to a vacant position
*   adjusting or modifying examinations, training materials, or policies
*   providing readers or interpreters
*   making the workplace readily accessible to and usable by people with disabilities

Succeeding In The Workplace provides a complete discussion of the law and outlines the details of other related laws that protect individuals with disabilities from school or work discrimination.

Disclosing a Disability: A Two-Sided Issue

Disclosing a disability is a complex issue. The decision should be given careful consideration.

Succeeding in the Workplace presents this as a two-fold issue. On the one hand, you are under no obligation to disclose your disability unless you require reasonable accommodations. The risk of disclosure is that, even if not intending to, the employer might "type"you as a person who is in some way "limited." This could affect your future with that employer.

On the other hand, if you need some type of accommodation, it might be in your best interest to know up front if the employer has a problem with that. For example, if you have a hearing disability, you would want to mention (once you are offered a job) that there is a telephone device that improves your hearing. This eliminates a negative issue. It is also helpful if you already possess the specific information required about the device, such as where it can be obtained and the cost, to put the employer at ease. Call the Job Accommodation Network at 800-526-7234 to obtain such information free of charge.

The way in which a disability is discussed can make or break an interview. It should be discussed in an upbeat, reassuring way to let the employer know that this is not going to negatively impact your performance in any way, nor is it going to cost the employer an unreasonable amount of money for the accommodation. Instead of spending the time defending the disability, it is vitally important to reassure the employer that the strengths you possess for the job are such that you are the right person for the job. Give examples of just how suited you are for the position and paint a mental picture for the employer.

Getting First-Hand Information

Getting first-hand information about the type of work you will be expected to do at a job can be very helpful. Talking to people about their work and asking them specific questions provides valuable information. Equally helpful can be observing others while they are at work. You can learn first hand how it feels to be in a given environment and at what pace the workers are going. Observing might include any of the following: job shadowing, internship, volunteering, work evaluation, job analysis, or work hardening.

For the individual with disabilities, all of these become extremely important reality-testing procedures. You might find that concerns you have about your ability to perform a job are real. Or you might discover that you would be able to manage effectively.

For people with disabilities it can be particularly important to gather first-hand information about a job. There are often private or governmental agencies that will assist in gathering the information derived through a Work Evaluation or Job Analysis. If the disability is severe and threatens to interfere with employment at a desired level, this option often provides essential information not gathered by any other method. The Rehabilitation Act of 1973 (RA) prevents discrimination against individuals with disabilities in education and employment, and provides access to the benefits of federal programs by federal agencies and federal grant and contract recipients. There are programs that assist individuals and allow them to enter or return to the workforce or educational setting with a disability, within the definition of reasonable accommodations. Once you have gathered all of this information you are ready to make your decision.

> You have the choice
> to live your life
> leading with your strengths
> or offering your challenges
> as excuses
> for your failures.

Summary

Regardless of what challenges or disabilities you may have, in looking for a career you should always start with your strengths. Review your skills in comparison to any functional limitations you may have. Employers are often willing to assist employees with special needs by making reasonable job accommodations. Disclosing a hidden disability to an employer should be done only after careful consideration. Gathering first-hand information about your compatability with specific work environments can be done through job shadowing, internship experiences, volunteer work, or a work evaluation program. Remember to lead with your strengths to find a job in which you will be fulfilled.

PEOPLE WHO LOVE THEIR WORK

Name: Mark D'Alleva

Hometown: West Bloomfield, MI

Job title: Hair stylist/Salon Owner

Basic tasks of the job: Beyond being a colorist, styling hair, make-up and image consulting, probably the most important part of this job is being able to listen and accurately interpret what clients are saying versus what they really mean.

Why I enjoy my work: This is a people job! It requires conceptualization skills. I get instant gratification when I have successfully helped an individual to feel better about him/herself. To see a big smile on the face of someone who arrived looking timid and fearful gives me great satisfaction. I enjoy problem solving with a client and reaching a positive outcome. There is a daily (and hourly) challenge in communicating with people, which keeps it always new and interesting.

Advice for those thinking about this type of work: Of course you need to be well-trained. In addition, it's a great idea to begin observing really good stylists near you, even while you are still in training. Learning the technical skills is essential, but getting "out there" watching successful role models is the way to pattern yourself after the best.

Chapter 12

ADDING TO
YOUR JOB SKILLS

Chapter Highlights

- As you saw in Chapter 3, identifying your skills is important in the career development process. Adding to your skill list should be a lifelong process.
- If you are not sure what field is best for you, sampling a class in a particular area might be a good way to decide if it is worth going further.
- Many resources near you can lead you to additional skill building.
- Learning a new skill or adding to existing ones ensures that you will remain a desired and marketable worker.

Skill Building: A Lifelong Process

You learned in Chapter 3 that prospective employers look for job applicants with the skills and experience necessary to perform a job well. Identifying your skills and abilities enables you to discuss what you can do to contribute to the workforce. The more you contribute, the more desirable you are to the employer. Even owning a successful business requires that you be more skilled than your competitors. In addition, those who reach their desired level of expertise in a career will want to continually upgrade their skills in order to remain on top of the demands of a constantly changing labor market.

What if you analyzed your skills in Chapter 3 and decided that you lack the degree of expertise required to do what you'd like? Or what if you realized that while you may have some skills in some areas, you could stand to improve in others? What can you do to acquire these skills?

The following are some classifications of help centers that might offer additional skills that could benefit you. There are many opportunities for skill building within your own community. While the array will vary from state to state, you can always start with your local librarian, a high school or college counselor, or a career counselor who can help you become familiar with what is available near you.

Community Resources

1. Vocational Technical Centers

Many school systems include Vocational Technical Centers that offer high school juniors and seniors an opportunity to learn about careers that require technical skills specific to a job. These centers offer classes during students' regular school days, but are usually held in separate buildings. This allows students to continue working towards high school graduation while also acquiring technical skills that could allow them to transition directly to a career after graduation. In addition, these centers provide a foundation on which to build technical abilities after high school. In many cases, mature adults are allowed to fill available slots in these programs, provided they fulfill the particulars of that center's requirements. The programs at these schools are career oriented and are primarily in the fields of business, real estate, banking, accounting, technology, personal services, health care, and trades.

Some centers include more academically based areas such as chemistry, library science, English composition and foreign language translation. Some programs may span as many as 240 careers and include preparation for such high-paying fields as dental hygiene, paralegal work, and aviation. Information about such programs can be obtained by contacting Peterson's Education Center at http://www.petersons.com/.

2. Continuing Education Programs

Continuing education programs are generally part of many communitys' efforts to provide "lifelong learning" to residents. These are designed to provide you with an opportunity to pursue a wide range of education or personal interests. You may wish to complete your General Educational Development (GED), obtaining skills in the areas of writing, social studies, science, literature and the arts, and mathematics. These are often free to citizens of the particular community in which they are found. In addition, there is usually a wide range of customized courses and seminars designed to enhance your specific and/ or overall skill level in such areas as management skills, professional development, computer applications, foreign languages, interpersonal communications, customer service, medical office management, automotive work, healthcare, and technology. Often included in this lineup are "fun" courses, such as flower arranging, recreation, financial planning and other "enrichment" courses. In addition to being stimulating and enjoyable, this classification continues your lifelong learning and offers further opportunity for building skills.

3. Military Options

High school counselors work with military service recruiters to provide appropriate referrals for military training. In addition to providing interpersonal "core" skills of discipline, problem-solving, organization, etc., a military career provides numerous opportunities to obtain specific career training both while in the military or following the service, with scholarships. More specific information can be obtained by checking websites like: http://www.lookingforwork.com/usmilitary.htm.

4. Community Colleges

Community colleges, which are supported financially by each state, offer a wide range of learning opportunities, at a reasonable tuition cost. Two-year programs are often available in such career areas as:

Applied Textiles	Electronics Servicing Technology
Architectural Technology	Electronics Technology
Automotive Service Technician	Food Service Management
Aviation Maintenance Technology	General Business
Building Technology	Industrial Media
Child Care Service	Liberal Studies
Climate Control Technology	Manufacturing Technology
Clinical Lab Technician	Media Illustration
Crafts	Office Information Systems
Criminal Justice	Office Information Systems-Medical Option
Computer Aided Design-Mechanical	Office Information Systems-Legal Option
Computer Information Systems	Wastewater Technology
Electromechanical Technology	

Certificate programs, which are usually less than two years, offer options such as:

Automotive Service	Heating & Air Conditioning/Refrigeration
Carpentry	Office Systems
Clinical Assistant	Practical Nursing
Corrections	Surgical Technology
Culinary Arts	Wastewater Treatment Plant Operator

The community college is often a great place for the adolescent who is not sure what to do next, the adult who wishes relatively short-term career training, or those who are returning to the learning arena to sharpen skills, transition into different areas or just learn about something of interest.

5. Vocational Rehabilitation Services

If you are an individual with a disability, you might be able to obtain training and skill building through your state Vocational Rehabilitation Services. You will have to meet with a Vocational Rehabilitation counselor to see if you quality, and then you will be assessed in terms of what skills might be needed to maximize your work potential.

Vocational Rehabilitation Services often pays for an individual to complete an appropriate training program, once it is determined that the goal fits. In addition, Vocational Rehabilitation Services offers support for accommodations that might be required once on the job and follow along if necessary to ensure career success. In accident cases, private vocational services for rehabilitation may be available through the related insurance company.

6. Community Support Services

If you have a particular disability, you will also want to contact the related community support agency to see if there are any opportunities for obtaining skills through them. Easter Seals, Council for the Blind, American Cancer Society, Alzheimer's Association and others provide support and funding for appropriate services. Often they can work hand in glove with Vocational Rehabilitation Services and other community agencies to do "case management" in assessing and providing help where needed.

7. Technical Skills Training

In addition to public services, there are often private companies that offer technical skills in specific areas such as:
Truck driving
Drapery and bedspread making
Cosmetology
Apparel alteration/tailoring
Industrial trades
Computer technology
Medical/dental assistants and technicians
Business careers

Looking in the Yellow Pages under "Schools" will lead you to many other ideas for specific training programs and technical trades.

8. Apprenticeships

Another source of skill building is the apprenticeship, an opportunity to obtain technical skills through watching and assisting a trained worker in a specific area, and attending in-school training. Depending on the field, requirements vary in terms of how many hours of each is needed. Generally, apprentices must be employed and work in the trade of their choice for 3-5 years and attend related classes. While apprenticeships are usually paid positions, the pay is at a much lower level than would be earned once the individual has completed all the requirements. Some examples of these programs are:

Asbestos (4 hours/week; 144 hours/year)
Brick Mason (4 hours/week; 144 hours/year)
Carpenter (4 hours/week; 144 hours/year)
Cement Mason (4 hours/week; 144 hours/year)
Electrician (152 hours/year)
Glazier/Floorlayer/Painting/Decorating (4 hours/wk; 160 hours/year)
Independent Electrical Contractor, IEC (4 hours/week; 144 hours/year)
Ironworker (4 hours/week; 144 hours/year)
Marble and Tile Setting (4 hours/week; 144 hours/year)
Plumber (6 hours/week; 216 hours/year)

9. Co-ops/Trainee Programs/Internships

Many high schools offer co-op programs, trainee programs, and internship opportunities to build skills. In a co-op program an individual attends classes half a day and then works in the community half a day obtaining job skills. A trainee program might include short-term courses in skills such as CPR, child care, medical assisting, office support and others. Internships offer extended opportunities to be present in the workforce in an area of interest. All of these are invaluable for gaining skills and provide a marked advantage for future employability.

School counselors can be extremely helpful in matching students to available co-op, trainee, or internship situations. In addition, individuals are often able to create their own situations, through direct contact with places of employment. This demonstrates initiative on the part of the individual and is often looked upon as a plus in terms of initial impressions. Trainee positions and internships are therefore possible with all age groups, including those looking to transition into "retirement," or the next chapter of their lives.

Summary

Adding to your skill list should be a lifelong process. You can never have too many skills. If you are looking to get into a particular area of work, you must possess the relevant skills in order to be competitive in today's job market. If you aren't sure what field is best for you, sampling a class in some of these areas might be a good way for you to decide if it would be worth going further. There are many places near you that can offer an opportunity to obtain additional skills. Learning a new skill or adding to existing ones ensures that you will remain a desired and marketable worker, now and in the future!

Part II

Finding a Job
Within Your Chosen Career

PEOPLE WHO LOVE THEIR WORK

Name: Arthur L. Robin, Ph.D.

Hometown: Birmingham, MI

Job title: Psychologist

Basic tasks of the job: (1) Help people with behavioral and emotional problems, particularly ADHD, eating disorders, and family conflict; (2) conduct research into new methods of helping people with behavioral and emotional problems and write about these methods; and (3) train young psychologists and physicians to be effective helpers.

Why I enjoy my work: It is very fulfilling to help others. It fulfills a basic human need. I enjoy finding out new knowledge from research and translating that knowledge directly into my clinical practice. There is infinite variety and a lot of challenges.

Advice for those thinking about this type of work: In these times of changing health care finances, you have to think very carefully about how you are going to make a living as a psychologist. It is increasingly difficult to earn a living from private practice, and hospitals and universities are also experiencing cutbacks. You have to be flexible, creative, and willing to work in a number of different settings over your career.

Chapter 13

THE CHANGING LABOR MARKET AND YOUR CAREER

Chapter Highlights

- The labor market is forever evolving. Being aware of labor market trends may influence the training or career selections you make.
- The Bureau of Labor Statistics of the U.S. Department of Labor is an excellent resource on trends in the labor market.

Labor Market Changes for the New Millennium

What changes can we expect now that we have turned the corner of the new millennium, and how will changes in the workplace affect you in your career search?

In November 1999 the Bureau of Labor Statistics, U.S. Department of Labor, provided information on the Labor Department's outlook for the workplace between 1998 and 2008. Over this ten-year period, total employment is projected to increase by 14 percent. The charts on the next pages indicate trends in the labor market by industry employment, job growth, and training requirements.

As can be seen in the chart on the following page, service-producing industries will account for virtually all of the job growth in the next several years. Jobs in health services, business services and social services, and in engineering, management, and related services are expected to increase. The only field that will add jobs in the goods-producing sector will be construction. There will be declines in manufacturing and mining with corresponding decreases in jobs.

The five fastest-growing occupations are computer-related occupations, commonly referred to as information technology occupations. Workers in the job force will be required to keep up to date with knowledge of computer skills, use of software applications, and use of new technology for communication. Computer engineer, computer support specialist, systems analyst, database administrator, and desktop publishing specialist are examples of occupations that are expected to grow very quickly. Other groups projected to grow faster than the average are executive, administrative, and managerial occupations; technicians and related support occupations; and marketing and sales occupations.

The 10 Fastest Growing Occupations, 1998-2008

Occupation	Employment*		Percent Change
	1998	2008	
Computer engineers	299	622	108
Computer support specialists	429	869	102
Systems analysts	617	1,194	94
Database administrators	87	155	77
Desktop publishing specialists	26	44	73
Paralegals and legal assistants	136	220	62
Personal care and home health aides	746	1,179	58
Medical assistants	252	398	58
Social and human service assistants	268	410	53

*Numbers in thousands of jobs
Source: *Bureau of Labor Statistics, BLS Releases New 1998-2008 Employment Projections, November 30, 1999. (Internet: http://stats.bls.gov/emphome.htm)

Among the industries projected to be the fastest growing from 1998-2008 are computer and data processing, health services, residential care, management and public relations, and personnel supply services. Refer to the chart below for a list of the fastest growing industries.

The Fastest Growing Industries, 1998-2008

Industry	Employment*		Percent Change
	1998	2008	
Computer and data processing	1,599	3,472	117
Health services	1,209	2,018	67
Residential care	747	1,171	57
Management and public relations	1,034	1,500	45
Personnel supply services	3,230	4,623	43

The Fastest Growing Industries, 1998-2008 (cont.)

Industry	Employment* 1998	2008	Percent Change
Miscellaneous equipment rental/leasing	258	369	43
Museums, botanical and zoological gardens	93	131	42
Research and testing services	614	861	40
Miscellaneous transportation services	236	329	40
Security and commodity brokers	645	900	40

*Numbers in thousands of jobs

Source: *Bureau of Labor Statistics, BLS Releases New 1998-2008 Employment Projections, November 30, 1999. (Internet: http://stats.bls.gov/emphome.htm)

Occupations showing the strongest decline in workers are related to agriculture (farmers), manufacturing, business and office. Fewer jobs will be available in the agriculture industry as new technology and larger machinery used to produce crops and livestock replace farm workers. Manufacturing will suffer considerably as production moves overseas and products are increasingly imported from abroad. New technology may decrease the need for people in occupations such as bookkeeping, accounting, and auditing. Secretarial jobs requiring typing and word processing may continue to decline.

As can be seen in the tables on the following pages, employment in all education and training categories that require an associate degree or higher is projected to grow at a faster rate than average. Employment will decrease for people with lower levels of education and increase for people with higher levels of training and education. While a four-year college degree may not always be necessary, employees who have vocational training and/or community college education will be much more competitive in the job market. For top jobs a four- year college education will still be best.

Other Trends in the Labor Market

The supply of workers (labor force) will increase by 12 percent from 1998-2008. This is slightly slower growth (10 percent) than the previous ten years. Due to the baby boom generation, the labor force age 45-64 will grow faster than the labor force of any other age group. The labor force age 25-34 is expected to decline, reflecting the decrease in births in the late 1960's and 1970's. Women will continue to enlarge their share of the labor force, which will grow more rapidly than men's share, increasing from 46 percent in 1998 to 48 percent in 2008.

Fastest Growing Occupations Covered
in the 2000-01 Occupational Outlook Handbook, 1998-2008

Occupation	% Change 1998-2008	Most significant source of training
Computer engineers	108	Bachelor's degree
Computer support specialists	102	Associate degree
Systems analysts	94	Bachelor's degree
Database administrators	77	Bachelor's degree
Desktop publishing specialists	73	Long-term on-the-job training
Paralegals and legal assistants	62	Associate degree
Medical assistants	58	Moderate-term on-the-job training
Personal care and home health aides	58	Short-term on-the-job training
Social and human service asssistants	53	Moderate-term on-the-job training
Physician assistants	48	Bachelor's degree
Data processing equipment repairers	47	Postsecondary vocational training
Residential counselors	46	Bachelor's degree
Electronic semiconductor processors	45	Moderate-term on-the-job training
Engineering, natural science, and computer and information systems mgrs.	44	Work experience, plus degree
Physical therapy assistants and aids	44	Associate degree
Medical records and health information technicians	44	Associate degree
Respiratory therapists	43	Associate degree
Surgical technologists	42	Postsecondary vocational training
Dental assistants	42	Moderate-term on-the-job training
Occupational therapy assistants and aides	40	Associate degree
Speech-language and pathologists and audiologists	39	Master's degree
Cardiovascular technologists and technicians	39	Associate Degree
Correctional officers	39	Long-term on-the-job training
Social workers	36	Bachelor's degree
Biological scientists	35	Doctorate degree
Ambulance drivers and attendants, except EMTs	35	Short term on-the-job training
Bill and account collectors	35	Short term on-the-job training
Physical therapists	34	Master's degree

Source: *Bureau of Labor Statistics, BLS Releases New 1998-2008 Employment Projections, November 30, 1999. (Internet: http://stats.bls.gov/emphome.htm)

Occupations Covered in the 2000-01 Occupational Outlook Handbook with The Largest Projected Job Growth, 1998-2008

Occupation	% Change 1998-2008	Most significant source of training
Systems analysts	94	Bachelor's degree
Retail salespersons	14	Short term on-the-job training
Cashiers	17	Short term on-the-job training
General managers and top executives	16	Work place experience plus degree
Truck drivers light and heavy	17	Short-term on-the- job training
Office clerks, general	62	Short-term on-the- job training
Registered nurses	22	Associate degree
Computer support specialists	102	Associate degree
Personal care and home health aides	58	Short-term on-the-job training
Teacher assistants	32	Short-term on-the-job training
Janitors and cleaners, maids, housekeepers	12	Short-term on-the-job training
Nursing aides, orderlies, and attendants	24	Short-term on-the-job training
Computer engineers	108	Bachelor's degree
Teachers, secondary school	23	Bachelor's degree
Office and administrative support supervisors and managers	19	Work experience in a related occup.
Receptionists and information clerks	24	Short-term on-the-job training
Waiters and waitresses	15	Short-term on-the-job training
Guards	29	Short-term on-the-job training
Marketing and sales worker supervisors	10	Work place experience plus degree
Food counter, fountain, related workers	12	Short-term on-the-job training
Child care workers	26	Short-term on-the-job training
Laborers, landscaping, groundskeeping	21	Short-term on-the-job training
Social workers	36	Bachelor's degree
Hand packers and packagers	22	Short-term on-the-job training
Teachers, elementary school	12	Bachelor's degree
Blue-collar worker, supervisor	9	Work experience in a related occup.
College and univeristy faculty	23	Doctorate degree
Computer programmers	30	Bachelor's degree
Adjustment clerks	34	Short term on-the-job training
Correctional officers	39	Long-term on-the-job training

Source: *Bureau of Labor Statistics, BLS Releases New 1998-2008 Employment Projections, November 30, 1999. (Internet: http://stats.bls.gov/emphome.htm)

Summary

Understanding labor trends can influence your career choices. It is important to keep up with these trends in order to take advantage of the most opportunities available to you. According to the U.S. Bureau of Labor Statistics, the five fastest-growing occupations are computer-related occupations, commonly referred to as information technology occupations. Occupations that show the strongest decline in the number of workers are related to agriculture (farmers), manufacturing, and business. Employment in all education and training categories that require an associate degree or higher is projected to grow at a faster rate than average.

PEOPLE WHO LOVE THEIR WORK

Name: Phyllis Levitt, MA LLP

Hometown: West Bloomfield, MI

Job title: MA Psychologist

Basic tasks of the job: Provide therapy to individuals, couples, and groups. Attend seminars in the field and administer intelligence tests and other psychological tests.

Why I enjoy my work: It is an extremely rewarding experience to help people see the options they have in their feelings, attitudes and behaviors that can change hopelessness, desperation and anxiety into strong emotional health. I learn as much from my interactions with my clients as I hope they gain from me.

Advice for those thinking about this type of work:
* Do volunteer work in mental health settings, support groups or areas that may be of interest. This will build your background and your experience and establish an impressive resume.
* Look into psychology and social work programs to see which ones are most compatible with your interests, and have recognizable licensing and accreditation.
* Attend workshops and seminars that could enhance your knowledge.
* Meet with practicing clinicians to learn about their procedures and skills.
* Read! Read! Read! Read everything you can get your hands on in the mental health field. Try to keep it current.

Chapter 14

THE INFORMATION INTERVIEW AND OTHER JOB INFORMATION RESOURCES

Chapter Highlights

- You can narrow your career search by using resources available in many libraries.
- An information interview is an excellent way to learn details about a job you would otherwise not learn by reading alone.
- Observing others at work in their jobs or working at a specific job can provide additional information to help you make a decision.

Read About Different Careers

Volumes of books and reference materials about career choices are available today. The amount of information can be overwhelming. The *Dictionary of Occupational Titles (DOT)* and *Occupational Information System (OIS)*, found in most libraries, are important sources of information.

As explained earlier, the *DOT* is a large reference book found in the Career Reference section of the library. It contains definitions of thousands of jobs, grouped according to similarity. The purpose of this dictionary is to define the tasks involved in the job. If the tasks don't appeal to the career seeker, then the search can stop right there. If the tasks are appealing or there is a question about whether this is a good match, it is necessary to go to the second reference, *OIS*.

The *OIS* is also found in the library. Usually computerized (sometimes it might be found on microfiche) this reference allows career seekers to learn about themselves or jobs. The *OIS* contains a short assessment, which takes less than 10 minutes for most people to complete. Based on your responses, a list of potential job matches is generated. You can then refer to the second section of the *OIS* and find out about the jobs themselves. Some of the information contained about different jobs includes:

- the specific tasks of the job
- the type of person who does best at this job
- the qualities necessary to do well at the job
- the environments in which people in this field work
- the statewide and national outlook for this job in the future
- the range of salary one can expect in this job
- the training and/or education needed
- the places to call or write for more information
- careers related to this one

After reading about a job in the *OIS* you may have a pretty good sense as to whether the job is appropriate for you to consider. Your next step is to try to find someone with the same or similar job and talk to them about it. This is not always easy to accomplish, but with a little resourcefulness and persistence you can usually find others in your community, or nearby, who would be willing to talk with you about what they do. However, you never want to form your impressions of a job by talking to just one person in a field. You may get a biased point of view. Try to find more than one person to talk to. The conversations you have with these people are called "information interviews." They are often the turning point in the career decision-making process.

Conduct Information Interviews about Careers You Want to Investigate

An information interview is a meeting in which you ask for job information, not a job. You may know of someone who is employed in a field that you are researching, or someone you know may be able to introduce you to someone else. The benefits of conducting information interviews are as follows:

- You may have preconceived ideas about what a job is like. You will get a better feel for the job than from any reading (though the reading should be done first).
- Talking with people about their jobs can provide you with realistic, first-hand information. Talk to at least a handful of people in several different careers. This will help you make better career choices.
- An information interview can be an opportunity to make some very helpful contacts.

Often, people will suggest names of other people who can provide you with further information.

- An information interview is a good way to check on and improve your interviewing skills. It allows you to present yourself in a non-pressured situation. You will learn useful information that you can use in an actual job interview.

Getting Started with Information Interviews

The first information interview is the hardest, but they do get easier. Here is a way to begin.

1. Identify the career (or careers) you wish to learn about.
2. Get a loose-leaf binder and a set of dividers. Label the dividers with the various career options you wish to research. Put all materials related to that option in the appropriate section of your binder.
3. Set up appointments with people you would like to interview. An appointment in person is best. This allows you to look around and see what the person's work environment is like. If you cannot visit the person in the work place try to conduct the interview over the telephone.
4. Conduct yourself in a professional manner. Arrive on time and dress for an interview. While this is not a "real" interview, the person you contact might choose to see you as someone to recommend for a position there. For this reason it is best to look professional at all times.
5. After the meeting, send a brief thank-you letter. This can be hand written and should be done on plain paper or on a thank you note card. Simply thank the person for spending time with you, remind her of something you most appreciated, and let her know you hope to be in contact with her again at some later point.

Knowing What to Say During the Cold Call

Because this is often a cold call, you will need to know exactly where you are headed in this conversation. Use this phone script. Modify it to fit your speaking style. Practice until you are comfortable with the content.

Information Interview Telephone Script

Hello. My name is _____

May I please have the name of the (person in charge of this job, or someone in the job itself).

Could I speak to M_____ (Not there?)

Is there a good time that I might call back? _____

Hello M_____My name is _____

I'm considering a career change, and _____

or

I'm _____yrs old and trying to decide on a career.

I've been advised that before I make a final move, it is best to contact some people in the field and talk to them about this type of work. Could we set up a 20-minute meeting where I could ask you a few questions?

(This is a place to create a "blurb" about yourself, when you are asked about your background. It usually starts with what training, education, or experience you've had.)

_____

_____

_____

_____

_____

_____

Conducting and Recording the Actual Information Interview

Below are the questions to ask during your information interview. Take careful notes during the interview. You may also want to ask permission to tape record the interview for future reference.

Information Interview Questions

1. Could you walk me through a typical day of what you do?

2. What do you like best about what you do?

3. What are the headaches of this type of work?

4. What would you recommend for someone just getting into this field?

5. What is looked for in the people hired for this type of work?

6. To what associations should someone in this field belong?

7. What training/education is required?

8. What salary range could I expect upon entering this field?

9. Could you give me the names of a couple of other people I might talk to?

   Name:_____ Phone: _____

   Name:_____ Phone: _____

   Name:_____ Phone: _____

   Name:_____ Phone: _____

Observe People at Work in the Careers You Have Selected to Investigate

The next step in finding out more about possible careers is to observe people at work doing the job you are considering. This can be done in several ways:

- You could simply watch someone doing the job, which is called "job shadowing."
- You could choose to do an unpaid or paid internship in the field as part of your education/training process.
- You could volunteer within the field for an established or open-ended period of time.

If you have a disability that could affect your job performance, you could try out a job with an evaluator or job coach giving you feedback. Several types of work evaluations can be done. These include:

1. a work evaluation, which tests you out in various job tasks and measures your performance and marketability;
2. a job analysis, in which an expert analyzes the tasks of the job to determine the degree of match between you and the demands of the job; and
3. work hardening, which evaluates your work performance with the goal of building up your tolerance and endurance to the demands of the job, bit by bit.

Summary

Once you have narrowed your search to specific careers it is a good idea to find out as much about a particular job as you can before you do your actual job search. Library resources such as the *DOT* and *OIS* provide a great deal of information on jobs in the U.S. These resources provide job descriptions, specific tasks of the job, the type of person who does best at this job, salary ranges, and the training and/or education needed to qualify for a particular job. In addition to these resources, it is very helpful to arrange to do an information interview with people already working at the job position you have in mind. You can get a first-hand look at the type of work they do on a daily basis and match their actual experiences with ones you anticipated from the job descriptions you read.

PEOPLE WHO LOVE THEIR WORK

Name: Tom Palmer

Hometown: Ypsilanti, MI

Job title: Loss Control Consultant

Basic tasks of the job: With a BS in Occupational Safety, tasks include visiting industrial customers and identifying where loss, injury or product hazard might occur. Information is used to help insurance companies for commercial businesses control and minimize the possibility of such occurrences.

Why I enjoy my work: I enjoy working out of my home, and yet meeting different people every day. It's always different and gives me an opportunity to travel. The travel time in the car allows me to listen to books on tape.

Advice for those thinking about this type of work: If you are thinking of this type of work, you should have good time-management skills because you will be on your own to complete paperwork and "loose ends" that need to be done.

Chapter 15

HOW DO PEOPLE FIND JOBS?

Chapter Highlights

- Finding a job can be a full-time job in itself.
- There are several methods a job seeker should use to find job opportunities. The most popular ones include sifting through "want ads" in the newspaper or trade publications, networking with others, making direct contact with companies, using the Internet, and using search firms or employment agencies.
- A combination of these methods will provide the greatest probability of success.

Conducting a High-Powered Job Search

The job market is always changing. New jobs are being created every day. People get promoted, retire, quit, relocate, die, or become disabled and cannot work. The jobs they previously held become vacant and new employees are needed to fill these positions. How many vacancies are there? The number is staggering. Richard Bolles estimates there are about 21,000,000 job vacancies per year.

Jobs become available even when we are in periods of economic depression. Although new jobs don't get created as easily, vacancies in existing jobs occur. So, imprint in your mind—there are jobs out there. There always are. All you need to do is find the ones that are right for you.

Before you do this you must set clear goals:
1. Based on the skills you have, you must know what type of job you want.
2. You must know the type of setting in which you want to work.

3. You must find the company in which you are most interested and sell it on your qualifications.

Methods Used in Job Searches

William was looking for a job. He had a new resume that was targeted to business management, a field in which he had seven years experience. Every Sunday morning William would go through the "want ads" in the local newspaper. He would circle all the appropriate ads and send out cover letters with his resumes. After four weeks of this type of search, William became discouraged. He had only heard from two of the employers, and of those, one was over an hour's drive from his house and the other sent him notification that the position had been filled.

William was right to comb through the "want ads" every weekend. In addition to informing him of available job openings, these ads also serve as idea triggers, suggesting other areas William might want to consider. However, limiting himself to using the "want ads" as his only method of job search will probably not get him the job he desires. In fact, less than one quarter of the people who search for jobs in newspaper ads actually secure one that is to their liking.

Conducting a job search is a little like fishing. Compare two fishing boat captains. One fishes all day long in one spot using one type of bait and one type of fishing tackle. He returns to the same spot every day regardless of his success. Another captain moves his boat from place to place, changing the bait and tackle to test where the fish are biting and what they are biting on. He records the results of his different efforts and determines the method that brings in the most fish.

Fortunately, job seekers have a number of different methods they can choose to find a job that suits them. Some, like William, rely primarily on "want ads" found in newspapers. Others network with colleagues, relatives, or friends to find leads. Some people contact companies directly (they may have seen them in their community or found them in the Yellow Pages). Going to a public or private employment agency or a search firm or using the Internet may also be useful for certain job titles. Each of these methods is described in more detail in the following sections.

Print Want Ads

Employers post job opportunities in the classified or "want ad" sections of newspapers and trade publications. Searching for a job by reviewing these ads can pay off. However, keep in mind that the vast majority of employers do not advertise their job openings in this way.

When scanning the ads don't focus only on the specific job title in which you are interested. Ads are listed alphabetically by title, but the work that interests you could be under a job title that is different from what you expect. For the best result, comb through all of the ads, once a week, in order to spot those ads that might appear in a different place, be called something else, or might be set off in a large block ad that is not in alphabetical order. Often we can learn more about what skills are required for a job, what salary range certain fields command, or how transferable skills might be utilized in a totally different field. One example of this might be the retired teacher who notices that large companies hire ex-teachers to teach in their New Employee Training Programs. This might be an idea that the ex-teacher has not thought of, but which can be marketed to other large companies.

To answer a "want ad," be timely. The average response time for a newspaper ad is 24 to 36 hours. You will probably be competing with many other applicants, so write your cover letter and mail it with your resume quickly. Employers placing "want ads" usually want to hire someone right away. Responses will be screened and only those applicants whose resume and cover letter seem attractive to the employer will be asked to interview. If there is no mention of salary in the ad, don't mention your salary requirements in the resume or cover letter. You may be screened out before being asked to interview. The interview, not your resume, is what the employer will rely on to make a final decision about hiring you. Qualifications listed in the ad should be presented in the cover letter and during the interview to confirm to the employer that you have the skills necessary to do the job you are seeking.

The print want ads can be helpful in giving you ideas about jobs. Consider the case of Mary.

Mary's Story

Mary was a 35-year-old laid-off English teacher. She taught grades 9-12 for 14 years and enjoyed the job with a fair degree of satisfaction. Her complaints about teaching were not unique. At the high school level, many students took Mary's class because they had to and not because they chose to, resulting in behavior challenges that took their toll on Mary's patience. While she wanted to return to teaching, she also entertained the idea of using the layoff as a good time to switch to something else. Looking through the Sunday want ads, Mary came upon a big block ad that read something like this:

> Wanted! Teachers!
> Local business establishment needs
> teachers to train new hires.
> Skills required include excellent presentation,
> communication, and interpersonal abilities.
> Salary commensurate with experience.
> Please send resume and salary requirements
> to:
> ABC Pickle Company
> 111 Vinegar Avenue
> Dill, New Jersey 00000
> No phone calls please.

Mary and her career counselor could have concentrated for the next 1,000 years and still would never have come up with a Pickle Company as a place for ex-teachers to work! However, this gave Mary other ideas:

- What other companies are large enough to do continuous training with employees?

- For what other types of workers might businesses provide training besides new hires?

- Where else might Mary contact directly to discuss her "excellent presentation, communication and interpersonal abilities?"

Mary did send a resume to the "ABC Pickle Company" but did not get hired there. She did, however, get hired fairly quickly at a large banking conglomerate that was setting up training programs at various levels within the bank system! The company admired her, not only for her outstanding skills as noted on her resume, but also for her initiative in contacting them. They presumed that Mary was able to problem solve beyond the norm.

Networking

Networking with friends, relatives, and colleagues can be one of the best ways to get leads on potential jobs. Ask each of these people if they know of someone hiring in the field you have chosen, or if they know someone who works in the field who may be contacted. Think of all the potential people in your network: classmates, co-workers, friends, relatives, casual acquaintances, people you go to for services (dental office, medical office, hairdresser, cleaners, etc.), religious leaders, e-mail buddies, people who share your hobby, etc.

Then develop a short "blurb" about yourself that you will recount when you meet with someone. It might be something like this:

"I'm currently looking for a position in business management. I have seven years experience at _____ where I was in charge of 13 people. I enjoyed working there and got excellent feedback from my employer. I was told that I have great organization and supervisory skills. If you know of anyone who might be looking for someone like me, I'd be glad to contact them."

You might keep some copies of your resume in your car in order to be able to leave a couple with a potential networking contact. Some people even have business cards made up with their name, address, phone number, e-mail address, and a short summary of their skills.

We have discussed the value of doing information interviews. In such an interview you discuss the type of work someone is doing so you can get a better idea of the job and its appeal to you. An information interview is a very good way to obtain facts about various career fields. The obvious by-product of doing information interviews is automatic networking. Such interviews give you the opportunity to meet people who are on the "inside" of whatever field you are hoping to enter. The person you interviewed may be willing to pass your resume along to one of her co-workers, or she may have an idea of where you might go to obtain a similar job. Most career counselors recommend that you not even bring your resumes to an information interview. However, it is perfectly fine to send a copy of your resume to that person later on, once your decision has been made about the type of position you are seeking. In your cover letter, remind the person that you came in for the information interview, thank her for the time she spent with you, and ask her about any openings in her company.

Direct Contact

Another great way to get a job is to decide which company you would like to work for and contact the company directly. It's that simple! Here is how it goes.

127

Go through the Yellow Pages of your local phone book—starting with the Index section. Highlight any categories that appeal to you and that might utilize your skills. Develop a short phone script that allows you to "cold call" a business and introduce yourself. You will either want to speak to the person who hires, such as the human resource specialist, or the person in charge of the position you would like to have. Don't leave messages, as they are seldom returned. Instead, indicate that you would be happy to call back later at a better time, and be sure that you get the name of the appropriate person. Such an introduction might sound like this:

"Hello. My name is William Careerseeker. I have seven years experience in business management where I was responsible for 13 people. I was told that I am highly organized and have excellent supervisory skills. I am hoping to utilize my detail-oriented abilities, working for a mid-sized company such as yours. Could we set up an appointment time when I could come in and drop off a resume?"

If you are told that there are no openings at this time, you should simply respond with: "That's ok and I understand. I would still like to come in, meet you and drop off my resume for any future needs that your company may have. I'm going to be in your area next week. Could I come by on Wednesday or Friday?"

It may sound aggressive, but it does give the employer the distinct impression that you are a person who gets "the job done." There is also a big difference between coming on aggressively and being "business assertive." The latter is direct without an offensive sting.

Internet

The Internet has provided us with an overwhelming number of work-related resources. A few of these are listed below:

- monster.com
- hotjobs.com
- headhunter.com
- careermosaic.com
- careercity.com
- careerpath.com
- job.sleuth.com
- collegerecruiter.com

These web sites allow you to research companies, learn of available job openings, and post your resume. While there are dozens of other web sites available for job seekers, they tend to come and go. Use the keyword "career" or "jobs" to pull up a multitude of currently functioning web sites.

Having said that, you should be cautious about what information you give out about yourself on the Internet. Good people utilize the Internet. Bad people do, too. When you post your resume on the Internet, you are providing ALL people with a great deal of personal information. Scams have been reported in which a job seeker was robbed at his home, at the exact moment that he was searching for a bogus interview location. Research the company for which you are completing an Internet resume. Give your email address rather than your physical address until you are certain that the information is going to the right place. You can use the local library to find out more about the company you are looking into. There are corporate year-end reports in large libraries that give vast amounts of information on public companies. Ask a librarian to help you search for such needed data.

Employment Agencies

There are four types of employment agencies you can turn to for help in finding a job: government employment agencies, private agencies, temporary work agencies, and agencies used by employers to locate individuals with specific qualifications.

Government employment agencies are called by different names (Public Employment Service, state unemployment office, job service agency, etc.). The Public Employment Service is a state-operated program that provides labor exchange services to employers and job seekers through a network of 1800 offices throughout the United States. The Public Employment Service has helped people and jobs find each other for over 60 years. They exist in many areas of the country and people often go to these offices to collect unemployment benefits. They usually have lists of jobs ranging from entry level to highly skilled positions, and their services are free. You can use the Internet to search for a job on the America's Job Bank site (www.ajb.dni.us/). America's Job Bank is a partnership between the U.S. Department of Labor and the state-operated Public Employment Service. The America's Job Bank's computerized network links state employment service offices to provide job seekers with the largest pool of active job opportunities available anywhere. It also gives them nationwide exposure for their resumes. The job openings and resumes found in America's Job Bank are available on computer systems in public libraries, colleges and universities, high schools, shopping malls, transition military bases worldwide, and other places of public access.

Private employment agencies can be found throughout the United States. Look in the Yellow Pages under "employment agencies" to find a listing in your area. As you go through this list the job titles in which an agency specializes, e.g., financial, data processing, business, advertising, etc., will become clearer. When you work with a private employment agency you will be expected to sign a contract that specifies the responsibilities of the agency and your obligations. Fees are always charged by the agency. Sometimes these fees are paid by you and sometimes by the company that the agency refers you to. Be sure to read all contracts carefully.

Temporary agencies are private employment agencies that focus on finding temporary jobs for people. They can be found in the Yellow Pages. These agencies are especially helpful for those who are relocating to a new city and who don't yet know which companies are best; to those who lack job experience and wish to learn about different environments; to those who have not yet decided on a career but need income; or to those who wish to remain without the responsibilities of a permanent job.

Employment agencies that are hired by companies to find qualified applicants are called recruiters or executive search firms. Employers retain these companies to find executives or technically trained individuals who possess the skills needed by the employer. Many of the prospective employees are already working at a job and have registered with the search firm in case another position becomes available. The search firm will also recruit employees with certain job skills by contacting them, even though the employee is not actively seeking to change jobs. The fee for this service is paid by the company that hires the search firm.

The More Methods of Job Searching You Use, the Better Your Chances for Success

It just makes sense that the more methods you use in your job search the more likely you are to find a position that is appropriate for you. Obviously there are a lot of variables to consider before signing on with a company—salary, location, job title and responsibilities, your qualifications, etc. You will want to have as many options as possible before you select a job. The best way to increase your options is to search as ambitiously as you can using as many different procedures as possible to identify prospective employers. One method alone may produce some results, but using a combination of the methods identified above will probably increase your choices.

Exercise 14.1

Below is a Job Hunting Strategy form you can use to lay out your job search plan.

What kind of job are you looking for?

_____

_____

_____

What skills do you possess that qualify you for this type of job?

_____

_____

_____

In what setting do you want to work?

_____

_____

What salary range are you interested in?

_____

What responsibilities would you like to have in your job?

_____

_____

_____

_____

List five strategies that you will use to find the job you want.

_____

_____

_____

_____

_____

_____

In a separate notebook keep a daily diary of your efforts to find the job you want. Use this notebook to keep track of how you have networked, including contacts you may have made through ads, on your own, or through employment agencies. Maintain a log of applications completed and information (resumes, cover letters, references, etc.) you have sent to prospective employers.

Summary

Hunting for a job can be a full-time job in itself. There are many strategies you can use to find a company that would like to hire you. Going through the "want ads" in a newspaper or trade newsletter can bring you excellent leads. Directly contacting companies and sending out cover letters and resumes may pay off as well. Using the Internet or employment agencies to locate jobs that match your skills and experience are also good methods to use in your job hunt. There are usually plenty of jobs available. The best way to find one is to use as many different strategies as possible to search for them.

PEOPLE WHO LOVE THEIR WORK

Name: Pamela R. Letterman, RN

Hometown: Monroe, MI

Job title: Creator/owner-Lifecrafters-Help for creating a life that works

Basic tasks of the job: Education, support, medication monitoring, treatment networking.

Why I enjoy my work: I am able to utilize my nursing skills to the utmost. It feels like I'm really practicing my profession, which emphasizes health. I am able to implement a "bigger picture" of what treatment really is, so people are encouraged and supported in taking responsibility for themselves. I see folks at all levels of experience with their ADD/ADHD, from the ignorant, to the experienced, to the stuck. I am building a view of treatment that appreciates stages of recovery. This comes out of the dialogs and experiences I have with my clients. They are great people.

Advice for those thinking about this type of work: You need to have your basic skills in place. Honor your interests that compliment what you are doing, no matter how disparate they seem. Respect the lack of obvious logic—it will come when you need it. Do not fall into the trap of either/or—allow yourself to integrate all of who you are into your life plan. Identify the parts that require outside help and/or support, and get it!! Hold the paradox of taking yourself seriously and having fun.

Chapter 16

PREPARING A JOB RESUME AND COVER LETTERS

Chapter Highlights

- Once you have selected a career field, you must prepare cover letters and resumes to let prospective employers know more about you.
- There are several different types of resumes you can prepare—chronological, functional, and combination resumes are the most common.
- In this high-tech age, there are electronic resumes that are both mailed and sent via the Internet. It's important to know how to prepare them.
- In addition to a resume, the job for which you are applying may require a portfolio of your previous work.

What Is the Purpose of a Resume?

Communicating your qualifications to prospective employers is the next most important step in your job search. This is usually done through resumes and interviews. A resume should tell an employer your qualifications for a specific job position. It should focus attention on your strengths and your accomplishments. Employers prefer to see people "on paper" before scheduling an interview. Therefore, if you don't pass the resume review stage of the hiring process you are not likely to get to the interview stage.

> **Resumes (lead to) Interviews (which lead to) Jobs**

A resume and the cover letter that accompanies it are the first documents that explain to your prospective employer who you are and why you are applying for a job in his company. Because they are an employer's first impression of you, it is important to prepare a resume and a cover letter that will have a strong impact on him. Remember, your goal is to get invited to a job interview. Your resume must sell you as competent, enthusiastic, and likeable—someone the prospective employer would like to interview for a closer look.

Your resume should focus on what the employer wants, not what you want. A resume that describes your background without indicating the specific qualifications you possess to competently handle the job is not particularly useful or impressive to an employer. Your resume should describe the skills, abilities, accomplishments, and work experience that you possess <u>and</u> that would be a perfect match for the job you are seeking. To create such a resume you need to know as much about the job as possible. By researching what it takes to do a specific job your resume practically writes itself!

As sensible as this sounds, it is not the way most people job search. They prepare the resume first and look for the right job next. As you have learned in the previous chapters, the reverse approach should be taken. Research the skills the job requires and prepare your resume to fit the job requirements.

Preparing a Strong Resume

Millions of job seekers prepare and send their resumes to prospective employers every year. Few have the impact necessary for an employer to be persuaded to take a second look at the applicant and request an interview. What makes the difference between a winning resume and one that is just so-so?

Put yourself in the employer's shoes for a moment. A large company may make it known that they are seeking candidates for one or more positions. They may advertise in newspapers, on their websites, with employment agencies, etc. Their advertisements may bring in hundreds of resumes, which must be sorted to find the most qualified applicants.

In today's high tech world, some large companies scan resumes, specifically looking for certain words. If you use these words it is assumed you have certain skills and your resume gets scanned into the "yes" pile. Without mention of these terms you might get scanned into the "no" pile and stay there. However, in most companies resumes are reviewed by someone at the company involved in the hiring process. Some resumes are immediately discarded because the applicant is clearly not qualified. Some have been eliminated because of lack of sufficient experience, or because something negative stands out (i.e. frequent job changes). A handful stay in the "yes" pile, and even a smaller number get called for a personal interview. Hopefully, your resume will stand out enough for you to make the final cut.

Here is What Your Resume Should Include

- Your resume should clearly communicate your major strengths—not just your educational achievements and your work history.
- Your resume should clearly communicate your objective—what you want to do for the employer. This may be the most important statement on your resume and it should stand out.
- It is often a good idea to include a "Summary of Qualifications" section after stating your objective. This contains a bulleted list of three to five of your qualifications. It helps the reader focus on the skills you could bring to the position.
- Employers generally prefer receiving one or two-page resumes (unless a curriculum vitae is specifically requested). Long resumes take too much time to read. A high-impact resume will be brief and to the point, containing enough information to persuade the employer to call you for an interview. If you have had a lot of jobs it is not necessary to list all of them. Only the ones most recent and relevant to the job you are applying for should be listed.
- Your resume may include special awards and training, particularly if they are relevant to the job for which you are applying.
- Your resume should not contain any reference to salary expectations. This should be discussed at the interview stage.
- Include references to hobbies or interests only if they strengthen your job qualifications.
- Specific references should be supplied at the time of the interview and should not be listed on your resume. Your resume may contain a statement that references will be available on request.
- Your resume should be appealing to the eye and should not be crammed with information. When formatting the resume leave plenty of white space, use bullets, and underline statements for emphasis.
- Select a good weight paper and appropriate color. You want your resume to have a "feel of importance." However, don't go to the extreme of using card stock or heavily textured paper. Conservative colors such as white, off-white, ivory, light tan or light grey for the paper with black, navy, or dark brown for the type are attractive.

- If your want your resume to have any chance at all of being taken seriously, always include a cover letter (more about this later).
- Personal information such as age, race, sex, marital status, and number of children is not appropriate for a resume.

Example:

Teresa found out, through information interviewing, that in order to be hired as a top-notch administrative assistant, one needs to be detail oriented, possess good interpersonal skills, demonstrate the ability to correctly prioritize work tasks, and be able to take initiative. The words "detail-oriented," "interpersonal skills," "ability to prioritize," and "taking initiative" all needed to appear in the upper third of her new resume to clearly show the match between her skills and the targeted job. Beginning the resume with a chronological listing of places where Theresa had previously worked (called a chronological resume) did not necessarily stress these skills adequately. A skill resume most clearly pointed out to a prospective employer not only where Teresa had been before, but also her capabilities. This was especially important for switching job environments from, for example, a hospital setting to a law office. By showing the transferable skills, Teresa stated that she was capable of exhibiting the abilities needed, regardless of the environment.

Chronological, Functional, and Combination Resumes

Your resume should be based on a clear understanding of yourself and what the prospective employer is looking for in a job applicant. The most common types of resumes are:

1. Chronological resume
2. Functional resume
3. Combination chronological and functional resume

Each type of resume has advantages or disadvantages. The type of job for which you are applying will give you clues as to which type you should send.

The Chronological Resume

Chronological resumes are the easiest to write and most commonly prepared. They contain a list of work experiences in reverse chronological order (most recent to least recent) and describe the responsibilities required in each job rather than the specific abilities, skills, and accomplishments you possess to perform the job well. This type of resume tells the reviewer what you did in the past, but tells little about what you can do in the future.

Advantages:
- Highlights a record of steady employment.
- Expected by many employers.
- Easiest to prepare.
- Highlights companies you have worked for that have a good reputation.

Disadvantages:
- Often does not focus on skills.
- Emphasizes job hopping.
- Emphasizes large gaps in your work history.

The Functional Resume

The functional resume emphasizes qualifications—skills and accomplishments as opposed to dates, positions, and responsibilities. The content focuses on the objective indicated at the beginning, the applicant's skills, and the prospective employer's job needs. It essentially tells prospective employers what you can do for them.

Functional resumes are very useful for individuals who do not have a great deal of work experience, for individuals who have job hopped, and for individuals who have large gaps in their employment history. A chronological resume would accentuate the fact that you have moved from job to job or have not worked steadily, which may not be to your advantage. Skill resumes are more difficult to prepare because you need a good understanding of both your skills and the skills that would interest a prospective employer.

Advantages:
- Emphasizes skills and accomplishments.
- De-emphasizes spotty job history or frequent job changes.
- Focuses on what you can do (future) rather than on only what you have done (past).

Disadvantages
- Is not familiar to employers, who may feel something is missing.
- Provides no opportunity to highlight certain employers.
- Offers no clear work history.

The Combination Resume

This combines the best characteristics of the chronological resume and the functional resume. The combination resume may be more difficult to write. It contains a brief employment history presented chronologically, and stresses skills and competencies, including job titles and dates. This type of resume allows you to stress your qualifications by work history in chronological and functional terms.

Advantages:
- Provides what employers are used to seeing—a work history as well as skills and accomplishments.
- Provides employers with dates in your work history so they can determine how long you have stayed at different jobs, and if there have been any significant gaps in employment.

Disadvantages:
- A little more difficult to prepare.

You must use your own judgement about which type of resume will work best for you. If you are uncertain about which type to submit, prepare all three and show it to friends, relatives, or colleagues for their opinions. For more information, there are books about creating resumes that can be found in the Appendix, and on web sites on the internet, such as:

http://www.careermosaic.com/cm/11online/11online8.html
http://campus.monster.com

Three Sample Resume Styles

The following examples illustrate the difference between a chronological resume, a functional resume, and a combination resume. Notice that the format is different. The functional resume is based upon resumes from a very useful workbook called *The Resume Catalog: 200 Damn Good Examples*, by Yana Parker (1988).

Chronological Resume Style

Ann Forester
10223 Neat Street
Berkeley, CA 94704
(555) 123-5678
AF@aok.com

Objective: **Position as Administrative Assistant**

Work History

1995-Present   ABC Corporation, Oakland, CA
Administrative Assistant. Set up systems for new
business accounts. Direct work of seven account
executives. Record all business in and out.

1993-1995   RCA Steam Engines, West Coast, CA
Secretary. Responsible for typing, filing, answering
phones, directing mail, etc.

1990-1993   Rainbow Building Corp., Santa Clara, CA
Office assistant. Arranged assignments and logged
them into work schedules. Quoted bids. Typed
proposals.

1989-1990   Tiger Stadium, Detroit, MI
Office assistant. Answered phones, bookkeeping,
typed programs, sent materials to printer.

Education & Training

1994   Associates Degree. Oakland Community College,
Oakland, CA
1991   Certificate-Business Systems. Oakland Community
College, Oakland, CA
1990   Diploma. Riverside High School, Oakland CA

References furnished upon request

Functional Resume Style

Ann Forester
10223 Neat Street
Berkeley, CA 94704
(555) 123-5678
AF@aok.com

Objective: **Position as Administrative Assistant**

Summary of Qualifications
- Responsible for the work of several people, keeping track of each
- Capable of multi-tasking without losing effective details
- Excellent follow-through skills
- Highly dependable and self-directed
- Received outstanding performance reviews from employers

Professional Experience
Administrative
- Successfully coordinated the work of seven account executives, responsible for recording all aspects of their sales.
- Organized new computer system to maximize efficiency and cut down on errors.
- Updated all records, setting up new filing systems for whole office.
- Developed plan for increasing turn-around time with account executives, resulting in more business each month.

Office Skills
- Demonstrated excellent bookkeeping and record-keeping skills.
- Prepared high quality reports and brochures.
- Quickly learned several business computer systems, training others on the staff in how to use them.

References furnished upon request.

Combination Resume Style

Ann Forester
10223 Neat Street
Berkeley, CA 94704
(555) 123-5678
AF@aok.com

Objective: **Position as Administrative Assistant**

Summary of Qualifications
- Responsible for the work of several people, keeping track of each
- Capable of multi-tasking without losing effective details
- Excellent follow-through skills
- Highly dependable and self-directed
- Received outstanding performance reviews from employers

Skills & Abilities
Administrative
- Successfully coordinated the work of seven account executives, responsible for recording all aspects of their sales.
- Organized new computer system to maximize efficiency and cut down on errors.
- Updated all records, setting up new filing systems for whole office.
- Developed plan for increasing turn-around time with account executives, resulting in more business each month.

Office Skills
- Demonstrated excellent bookkeeping and record-keeping skills.
- Prepared high-quality reports and brochures.
- Quickly learned several business computer systems, training others on the staff in how to use them.

Work History
1995-Present	ABC Corporation, Oakland, CA
	Administrative Assistant
1993-1995	RCA Steam Engines, West Coast, CA
	Secretary

1990-1993	Rainbow Building Corp., Santa Clara, CA
	Office assistant.
1989-1990	Tiger Stadium, Detroit, MI.
	Office assistant.

Education & Training

1994	Associates Degree. Oakland Community College, Oakland, CA
1991	Certificate-Business Systems. Oakland Community College, Oakland, CA
1990	Diploma. Riverside High School, Oakland CA

References furnished upon request

Notice that the functional resume stresses what Lisa can do, rather than where she has been. This type of resume is most often used when there is a reason to omit the work history—such as several short-term employment positions, or a "spotty" work record. While this does highlight skills and abilities, it is generally thought to trigger questions in the prospective employer's mind in terms of what the job-seeker might be hiding.

Electronic Resumes

We are living in an era of rapidly changing electronics. More and more companies are using electronics in their screening processes to reduce paperwork in hiring new employees. Electronic resume scanning is primarily used by large (5000+ employees), and medium size (500-5000 employees) organizations to screen and sort applicants by qualifications. It is projected that 80% of medium-to-large-sized organizations will be using electronic resume screening by the year 2000. They use scanning devices to eliminate job aplicants who are not as appropriate for their needs as others. They assume that if you are applying for a job, you will include certain "key words" in your resume. If those "key words" are there, your resume will get scanned into the "yes" pile. If not, your resume gets scanned into the "no" pile, and you may never hear from the employer again.

In order to know what "key words" you need, there are two things you might consider when creating your resume:

1. When you researched this job using the *DOT* or *OOH*, what specific words were connected with this career? Be sure to use those specific words in your resume, in the

upper third section of the paper, using the functional or combination resume. You may want to include those key words in your objective at the top, as well as in the Skills and Abilities section that follows.

2. When answering an ad that was posted in a newspaper or on the Internet, what specific words were used to describe what the employer is seeking in an applicant? Those words become the key words that you want to be sure to include in your resume.

How do you know if your resume will be scanned? You don't know for sure. However, if you are applying to a large company, there may be a greater chance that they will utilize this type of software than if you are applying to a small, family-owned company. In either case, it is always important to include in your resume those "key words" that are specific to the job. That way you will ensure that you will be scanned "in" or will be considered for an interview.

The Internet Resume

If you contact the many on-line websites that allow you to post your resume, you will need to prepare your resume appropriately. The formats are usually the same: the chronological, functional or combination resumes. Because each computer is different the output might be different. That is, what you have sent--the spacing, bolding, italics, etc.--might not come across when the resume is received. Therefore, it is best, when sending your resume via the Internet, to keep it as clean as possible in terms of spacing and lines. Don't expect to use bold and italics to make your statements stand out. Use enough spacing so that whatever you want to stand out is clearly visible. Use tabs instead of your space bar to indent. In addition, follow up your electronic resume with hard copy, whenever possible, in order to provide the employer with a neat, well-presented version.

Cover Letters

If a resume is to be taken seriously it needs to be accompanied with a cover letter. The purpose of the cover letter is to introduce yourself to a prospective employer. It should be written in a way that grabs the attention of the reader. The cover letter doesn't need to be long, but it should draw attention to what you want noticed most about your qualifications.

In general, a cover letter is made up of three paragraphs. Paragraph one states why you are writing. You might start with a statement such as, "In reference to your ad in the *Detroit Free Press* of Sunday, January 2, 2000, for the position of Administrative Assistant, enclosed please find a copy of my resume for your consideration."

Paragraph two points out something from within the resume that you want the reader to notice. It might say something like, "As you can note from my resume, I have more than nine years experience as an Administrative Assistant, where I demonstrated strong detail-oriented skills, excellent interpersonal abilities and the ability to take initiative when necessary. I'm a self starter and believe that my skills match your requirements very well."

Paragraph three states what you hope will happen next, such as, "I look forward to speaking to you further about the position you have open. I encourage any questions you may have regarding my qualifications and background." As a backup, it is recommended that you end the letter by saying you will get in touch with the prospective employee to make sure he received the resume.

Cover Letter Checklist

____ include your telephone number, fax number, e-mail address, and physical address
____ include the date above the inside address
____ include some industry terms
____ limit letter to one or two pages
____ proofread for spelling and grammar errors
____ have someone else proofread it
____ do not handwrite
____ send in envelope that matches cover letter paper (unless mailing in large envelope without folding)
____ make reference to your skills and qualifications for the job
____ include statement at end indicating you will follow up to see that the cover letter and resume were received
____ do not use a generic greeting (Dear Sir, Dear Madam, etc.); address letter to a specific person
____ avoid using abbreviations and acronyms
____ do not include your photograph
____ make sure the person who reads the letter knows why you are writing, what you want, and what your qualifications are

Putting it all together in a business letter form, the cover letter might look something like this:

Mr. John Eager
222 Somewhere Blvd.
Outonalimb, NM 00012

January 2, 2000

Ms. Susan Screener
1234 Wannawork Ave.
Desired, NM 00012

Dear Ms. Screener,

I am writing regarding the ad you placed in the Sunday, January 2, 2000, want ads for the position of Administrative Assistant. Enclosed please find a copy of my resume.

As you can see from my resume, I've been told that I possess excellent detail-oriented, interpersonal and self-starting skills. I can work independently and prioritize well. I have many examples of these skills that I would be happy to discuss with you during our interview. Also, I possess letters of reference that support these statements and I look forward to sharing them with you at that time, too.

Thank you for your consideration. I look forward to answering any questions you may have at the interview. I will call your office next week to make sure you have received this.

Very sincerely,

John Eager

Letters of Recommendation

A letter of recommendation is a letter you've asked for, in which the writer states what he sees are your outstanding strengths. Letters of recommendation can be obtained from many sources. Employers are in a wonderful position to comment on skills, abilities, and demonstrated accomplishments related to the workplace. Employers are not the only source of letters of recommendation. Other letters may come from co-workers, immediate supervisors, support staff, business owners, partners, individuals who have known you for a very long time, neighbors who comment on cooperative tendencies, friends who write professional letters, and teachers who know you well.

How should letters of recommendation be used?

Most employers do not expect letters of recommendation to be sent along with the resume. These are often asked for later in the screening process. However, sometimes it may be helpful to send in three letters of recommendation with your resume. A good balance might be to send in two professional letters and one personal letter. Then, by including "References furnished upon request," at the end of a resume, you allow the interviewer to ask for additional sources, if needed.

Is it annoying to people to ask them to write a letter of recommendation?

You might think that your request for a letter is annoying. Actually, most people are more willing to construct a letter at their leisure than they are to write a letter on the spot, without warning. Even with prior warning, some people resent being called and asked for the recommendation on the phone. They worry that they may say something wrong or even illegal (see Chapter 16). The result can even be that they seem suspicious because they are nervous. The caller checking on a reference may worry that the previous employer is trying to hide something negative. It is far better to give someone the opportunity to think about what to say and how to say it in advance.

What if you didn't do a great job?

What if your former employer doesn't want to write a recommendation letter for you? If someone is reluctant to provide you with a letter of recommendation it is usually because the person doesn't know what to say, or has some misgivings about signing a letter of recommendation. In either case, it is helpful if you frame the request this way:

"Would you be willing to write a letter of recommendation for me in which you comment on what you view as my strengths?"

This wording puts the emphasis on your perceived strengths. This is not the same as asking for an across-the-board recommendation that says he thinks you should be hired. A letter of recommendation could even be written by an unhappy boss who feels you are better off somewhere else! The letter comments on strengths, not weaknesses.

148

Portfolio

A portfolio is a visual packaging of items, such as a scrapbook, a loose-leaf binder, or presentation board, that illustrates your abilities. Some people choose to create extra portfolios to leave with the prospective employer. Others simply take their one-and-only portfolios along on interviews.

For some jobs a portfolio is important if not essential. Most commonly, portfolios are used for interior design, home remodeling, drafting, engineering, sewing, teaching, artistic work, and other vocations that generate work that can be demonstrated through pictures or samples.

Presenting a portfolio can give you an advantage over other candidates. To create a quality portfolio, you want to start as early as possible in your career, saving items that might support your positive claims. Photographs are one way to accomplish this. Clippings of newspaper articles might be another. Samples of work might be effective and could be arranged in a three-dimensional way to impress the interviewer with your initiative, creativity, and competence.

If your portfolio is too large, the employer can't sample much of it during the interview. You could drop it off prior to the interview, or you could offer to leave it there afterwards. Either way, it can be utilized during your attempt to answer the all-important question of why are you perfect for the position! Whether or not a portfolio is an appropriate tool for you depends upon the area of work. Done tastefully, it can be used with little risk of offending in nearly all types of job interviews.

Getting the Resume to the Right Person

Keri came into career counseling totally frustrated. She claimed she had done everything in her power to get a job and nothing worked. When asked about her methods of finding a good job, Keri quickly answered by saying, "I've sent out 120 resumes in the past three months, and so far nothing has come about!" Further questioning revealed that Keri had sent most of the resumes out in response to newspaper ads, and the rest were sent out unsolicited. It was no wonder she was frustrated. While she felt like she was being productive, she had actually chosen the two most ineffective methods of getting a job.

This is not to say that sending out resumes or answering want ads is a waste of time. However, statistics show that these are not the most efficient ways to find the best job. You should never feel that you are limited to answering ads in the newspaper for your job search. In fact, while the newspaper is enormously helpful in many ways, it is the least likely place to get the job of your dreams.

149

Most unsolicited resumes end up in the wastebasket. Even if a resume is interesting, if it isn't expected, an employer is apt to toss it out just to survive the growing pile that develops on his desk. Sending unsolicited resumes is a horrible waste of time and effort for such a poor return on outcome. A much better approach is to call the place of employment and attempt to speak with the person you hope would read your resume. While it takes some practice, the return on the effort is excellent. Here's how that conversation might sound:

Job Seeker: "Hello, Mr. Smith. This is J.J. Seeker. I have had recent training on several computer programs and I have been told that I am a conscientious, hard-working person. I'm hoping to find a job as a computer trainee and would really appreciate an opportunity to stop by, meet you, and leave my resume with you."

Mr. Smith: "Well, Mr. Seeker, I'd hate to have you come all this way because at the moment there are no openings for a computer trainee. You could mail your resume to me and I'll keep it here should something open up."

Job Seeker: "Thank you very much, Mr. Smith. It's no trouble for me to stop over there. In fact I'll be right near there on Thursday or Friday. Which day might be better for you?"

Mr. Smith: "Remember, now, there aren't any openings at this time. Just so you understand."

Job Seeker: "I understand. I'd just like an opportunity to meet with you and let you know about me in case any future openings come up."

Mr. Smith: "OK then. How about Thursday at noon?"

Job Seeker: "That would be just great. I'll look forward to seeing you then."

Now while every conversation won't go exactly as this one did, the basic idea will remain the same. Sometimes you might be told that, in fact, there IS a job opening and to come right in and fill out an application. Sometimes you might be asked to mail the resume and you will be called to set up an interview. All of these scenarios are good ones and far better than doing a blind mass mailing that would end up in someone's wastebasket.

Some Additional Tips for Sending Resumes

- Use a 9 x 12 envelope rather than a #10 envelope. Larger envelopes get more attention and your resume will arrive without being folded. You may also consider sending the resume in a colorful next-day delivery envelope. It may get more attention.
- . Type the name and address on the envelope, rather than writing it by hand.
- Use a nice looking stamp on the envelope rather than postage by meter.
- Fax or e-mail your resume only when requested to do so.
- If requested, submit your resume on the company's web site.

Following Up on Your Resume

It is always a good idea to follow up within three to five working days after you have sent your resume and cover letter to a prospective employer. The purpose of the follow-up call is to confirm that the right person in the company received the resume and to find out when you might be contacted to learn the status of your resume. If you get voice mail when making your follow-up call leave a brief, positive message as to who you are and why you are calling. If you have trouble getting through to the right person you may have to make several follow-up calls spaced over a few days. Always be upbeat and enthusiastic. The person you are calling may have been very busy and unable to return your call.

Structuring Your Job Search

Marla had her entire family believing that she was doing everything in her power to get a job, yet it wasn't happening. She was looking in the paper on Sunday and reading the want ads. She usually found between one and three ads that caught her eye, and she answered them. Then she would wait for a response. As the days went by Marla got depressed and lost faith in herself and her skills. "Nobody wants to hire me" circulated through her head and dominated her thinking.

Marla was sabotaging her job search without knowing it. She was attempting to plant one or two seeds (contacts) and wait for those seeds to grow into a job. This is the most painful, self-defeating way to get a job. It forced Marla to imagine being in a freeze pattern until someone out there freed her from it. She would have done much better to have been pro-active and planted lots of seeds, thereby enhancing her chances of getting a job. She needed to structure her job search by planning ahead, starting each day with a list of whom to contact, sending out letters and resumes, and setting up interviews. Each day should have ended by planning for the next day's contacts.

Supporting the Process with a Coach

Job coaches are specially trained people who provide direction and support for people who are seeking jobs. A coach can meet with you, listen to your career goals, and then set up a plan to support you each day as you work towards the goals. Coaches of this sort can be found on the Internet. Just type in the keyword "Coach" for information on job coaches and/or executive coaches. Once thought to be only for the severely disabled, coaches today are utilized by many high powered individuals, who recognize that just as a talented ball player benefits from coaching, so would all people who set goals for themselves. Often a coach can support you in your job search by phone or e-mail.

Summary

After selecting a career field and identifying jobs within that field that interest you, you must prepare cover letters and resumes that will impress the prospective employer enough to invite you to interview. Resumes describe your education, work history, qualifications, and skills. They can be chronological, functional, or a combination of each. To give yourself maximum advantage over the other candidates, know about electronic resumes and how to create them for a professional presentation. Many of the Internet resources for career seekers, mentioned in the References and Resources section of this book will further help you design a resume that works for you. You must make certain that your resume gets into the hands of the hiring decision maker. Follow up on your resume to determine the status of your inquiry. The next step, if your resume passes muster, is the interview. This will be discussed in the following chapter.

PEOPLE WHO LOVE THEIR WORK

Name: Joyce Lane Ginsberg

Hometown: Bloomfield Hills, MI

Job Title: Professional Advocate for Special Education

Basic tasks of the job: Evaluate needs of the student, make an educational plan (including academic, social, emotional, and physical needs), assist in obtaining optimal accommodations and services under federal and state special education laws.

Why I enjoy my work: It is satisfying to see individuals become more productive and successful.

Advice for those thinking about this type of work: You need to be familiar with and know Special Educaion law and have some background in psychology or education.

Chapter 17

INTERVIEWING BETTER THAN YOUR COMPETITORS

Chapter Highlights

- Resumes tell the prospective employer about you on paper. Interviews show her who you are. It is important to make a good impression during the interview, so preparation is essential.
- You should have first-hand information about a job from doing previous information interviews. This will help you be aware of the characteristics employers are looking for when they hire people for that job.
- Interviewees are generally asked four types of questions. In responding to these questions you should focus on your strengths and have a positive attitude, not only about yourself, but about former employers and co-workers. Be prepared to answer all types of questions about your personality, past experiences, and current skills.

Four Categories of Interview Questions

There are only so many ways that interviewers can word questions necessary to properly screen candidates. Interview questions usually fall into one of four categories:

1. Questions to get you to speak openly and formulate ideas
These are open-ended questions designed to see how you formulate an idea and carry

it through. (i.e., "Tell me a little bit about yourself," or "What are your goals?") Through these questions, the interviewer wants to see if you can formulate a complete thought and develop it.

The employer is trying to decide whether or not you can take a rough idea and mold it into a concept that has a beginning, a middle, and an end. Don't ramble. Come to the end of your thought and stop speaking. People tend to become uncomfortable with silences, but rambling can get you into trouble. Finish your statement, relax, and wait for the next question. If you have already done information interviews you probably know what the optimal candidate looks like. You might say something like this for each of these examples:

* In this type of work, I think I am the kind of person you are looking for because...
or
* I have started to think about short- and long-term goals. I have some personal goals and several professional goals. I hope to continue to keep improving my skills throughout my career.

2. Questions to determine if you will take negative bait.
Many questions are designed to see if you will take the negative bait—that is, to see if you are a negative-type person (i.e., "What is the worst job/boss you've ever had?", "Describe what kind of person frustrates you," or "What is your greatest weakness?")

All of these questions hold out the potential for you to fall into "interview quicksand"! Once you venture into one of those areas, you fall in and have to spend several minutes trying to surface. If you begin to describe a worst job/boss, you may be illustrating how you gossip about others. If you go on and on about a person who frustrated you, what are you really indicating? That you are a negative, easily frustrated individual? Why would anyone want to hire you?

Does this mean that you should lie? Definitely not! Be truthful, yet tactful. It is important to tell the truth—always. But let's face it, a job interview lasts about 30 minutes, on average. At the start of the 30 minutes, the interviewer knows nothing about you. When you leave, what would you like him to know? If you only have 30 critical minutes to convince him that you are the right person for the job, don't take up valuable time with negativity.

Instead of being negative, you might respond like this:
* We've all had jobs and bosses that we've liked better than others, but I do try to make

the best of every situation and remain professional. I've even become pretty good friends with some former bosses.

- The kind of person that frustrates me is probably the same kind that frustrates you—someone who doesn't take pride in his work or who plays unnecessary games instead of doing his job correctly.
- I'm not saying that I'm a perfect person. I haven't met too many perfect people yet. But I can honestly tell you that I don't think I have any weaknesses that affect my work! I do have several strengths that I think would add to my working here, however...

Keeping the tone of the interview positive makes you a more attractive candidate.

3. Questions specific to your line of work
There is no substitute for knowledge of one's job. It is important to have enough knowledge of what will be required once on the job to adequately convey to the interviewer that you thoroughly understand and are able to fulfill the requirements of the job.

It is essential that you select specific examples to clearly illustrate that you are the right candidate. Describe situations where you have previously demonstrated an important skill and the positive outcome that resulted. If at all possible, plan to give the results in some graphic way. For example, it is weaker to say, "I was an excellent salesperson last year!" It is much stronger and more impressive to say, "My sales for last year topped $380,000, which exceeded my company's goal of $300,000!"

4. Questions to see what kind of person you are
Sometimes the interviewer simply wants to learn about your personality. Career candidates are often so intent on being professional that they are stiff and rigid. There is a big difference between remaining professional and being too stuffy. In order to get a broad picture of you an interviewer may ask you about your hobbies, interests, types of books you read, etc.

Preparing from Sample Interview Questions

Here is a list of interview questions to think about. Never try to memorize your response. However, it is a good idea to jot down a word that will trigger ideas for your answer. The first and last question can be thought through as a "package idea" that can be inserted when the time is right. Open with some clear structure and end with a positive summation.

Sample Interview Questions

Below each question is a suggestion for how to approach your answer. It is important to note that this is not an attempt to be redundant or dishonest. If the interview is a brief selection process of relevant information to share, make sure your answers are honest and reflect why you are the best candidate for the job.

1. Tell me about yourself.
   Stress your relevant skills for the job. Plan a beginning, middle, and end.

2. What are your strengths/weaknesses?
   Make strengths relate to the job. Choose to discuss an irrelevant weakness and turn the conversation back to positives.

3. Describe the most challenging work situation you ever had and the outcome.
   Choose one with a positive outcome. Be as specific in your example as possible.

4. What type of boss do you prefer?
   You rarely get to choose your own boss, so don't describe what you "need" to be happy. Show that you strive to get along with everyone.

5. Describe the worst work situation you ever had.
   Select a situation that you learned from, or avoid the question altogether, as in, "I've really learned a lot from even my least favorite situations! I've gained knowledge as I've gone along..."

6. Describe a work situation that you wish you had handled differently.
   Be careful not to select damaging examples. Keep positive and choose something that turned out all right but next time could be even better.

7. What do you hope to be doing in five years? ten years?
   The interviewer is looking to see if you intend to hop around or move on. Stress your personal goals instead of where you hope to be. Example: I hope that in five years I'll be even more efficient at what I do and will have learned more. You could also discuss hobbies you'd like to take up in five or ten years.

8. Describe your favorite work situation and why.
   Don't indicate that you enjoy work most when you're not working!

9. Defend the capabilities listed on your resume.
   Have some concrete examples handy of your most relevant capabilities.

10. In your last job, what made you the most proud?
    Don't be afraid to boast of your accomplishments. If you feel awkward doing that, start with, "I've been told that..."

11. What do you hope to improve upon as you continue in your career?
    Similar to #7.

12. How would people who have worked with you describe you?
    Select good examples to go with the adjectives.

13. Why do you think you'd be good at this job?
    What can you bring to this job that someone else might not be able to? What makes you special?

14. What are your job goals? Life/personal goals?
    Be sure to indicate team-oriented goals, rather than aggressive, personal job goals. Life/personal goals demonstrate much about our personalities.

15. What do you expect your references would say about you?
    Hopefully, you have already contacted your references and/or have letters of recommendation handy.

16. Why did you leave your last job?
    If the reason is negative, look the interviewer right in the eye and calmly explain. Otherwise, keep your answer as positive as possible.

17. What are your hobbies?
    What you choose to do in your spare time tells a lot about you as a person.

18. What frustrates you on a job? How do you communicate this frustration?
    The answer is similar to question #5. Stay open, calm, relaxed, and positive.

19. Do you have any questions for me?
    Always go in with some questions written down. If they've been answered, indicate that by saying something like, "I did have some questions, but during the course of this interview you've answered them all. I hope I can call you if I think of any later..."

20. We are going to hire one person out of 10 candidates. Why should that be you?
    This type of question usually comes at the end of most interviews. It might be worded

differently or it might not even be stated. The idea, however, remains the same. This is a good time for a summation that clearly states the match between what you know the position calls for and your skills, abilities, temperaments, etc.

Dressing for an Interview

As a general rule, you should always go to an interview dressed one step up from whatever you would be wearing on the job. How do you know how to dress on the job? You may get some ideas from having done information interviews at similar job sites.

Dressing for an interview—males:
If it's a T-shirt and jeans job, wear a button-down shirt and khaki pants.
If it's a button-down shirt job, wear a tie.
If it's a shirt-and-tie job, wear a sport jacket.
If it's a sport-jacket job, wear a suit.
Avoid earrings, wild colors, styles, etc. You will be safer with more conservative attire.

Dressing for an interview—females:
If it's a T-shirt and jeans job, wear a blouse and skirt or slacks.
If it's a blouse-and-slacks job, wear a skirt and jacket or sweater.
If it's a skirt-and-jacket job, wear a suit with a skirt.
Avoid heavy makeup, excessive jewelry, wild colors or styles of clothing. You will be safer with more conservative attire.

Other Hints and Tips for a Great Interview

1. Always arrive early enough to sit and relax, use the restroom, look over your resume, or recall your interview preparation.
2. Don't chew gum or drink beverages, as they can spill when you're nervous!
3. Come prepared to ask some questions. Make these relevant to the duties and responsibilities of the job, as opposed to questions about your benefits, vacations, breaks, etc.
4. Don't ask about the salary. It's considered poor business tact. Once you're offered the job, you are welcome to discuss the issue. Also, remember that, with information interviews completed prior to "real" interviewing, you already know the salary range, so you have some bargaining leverage.
5. Don't be defensive about having to behave according to proper interview form. Employers aren't looking for robots. They are looking for a great match, just as you are. If you don't appear to understand the interview game, chances are you won't

understand the workplace game.

6. Bring a portfolio with you if it is relevant.
7. Try to understand the time line before you leave. That is, when will the decision be made for this position? That information will allow you to follow up by phone, and ask about the status of the opening. (Don't make a pest of yourself, but one follow-up phone call is appropriate if the time line has passed.)
8. Write a thank-you note following the interview. It can be short and handwritten. It should consist of three paragraphs.

Sample Thank-you Note

Paragraph 1

(A thank-you sentence.) Thank you for your time and kindness in our interview today, January 1, 2000. I enjoyed speaking with you about the opportunity to work at your company.

Paragraph 2

(A reminder of a positive.) As I indicated today, my experience at ABC company allowed me to learn the skills necessary to do this job. I believe that I would make an optimal candidate for the position.

Paragraph 3

(What you hope will happen next.) I look forward to further discussion about this exciting opportunity. Please feel free to call with any additional questions you may have.

Send the thank-you note immediately! It illustrates your attention to detail as well as your thoughtfulness.

Jared's Story

Jared had done everything right. He took the time to think about how his interests, abilities, and personality preferences relate to his career search. He prioritized the things he wanted to get out of a job. He had a better focus on his career goals. He went to the library and read about different career options. He was shocked that the research turned out to be fun for him. He especially enjoyed doing the information interviews, once he had some practice and no longer felt awkward. He even managed to observe people at work in his new field of choice. He was ready to forge ahead.

Jared's new resume was filled with great examples of what he could offer to the job. He was proud of the resume and received positive feedback from prospective employers. Jared appeared to have no trouble getting job interviews. That's when his nightmare began.

Jared had been "let go" from a previous job. While he had done an outstanding job in his capacity as an employee, Jared was responsible for picking his children up from school at 3:00 p.m., a duty that consistently made him unavailable for staff meetings. In the meantime, Jared's employer chose him as the necessary "cut" that needed to be made in his staff. Jared was devastated, and although he felt enormous frustration about it, he chose to prepare for future interviews by hoping he would not be asked any questions regarding why he left his last job. The result was that, although Jared went on many interviews, he wasn't having luck getting job offers. Something had to change.

Identifying the Problem

When someone is having trouble getting a job for which he is suited, it is important to determine where the process is breaking down. If Jared had not received positive feedback on his resume, it would have been necessary to find out what his resume was missing. However, since Jared was getting called to set up interviews, it appeared that his problem had something to do with what was going on within the interview.

In career counseling, Jared was given a video-taped mock interview. He dressed as he would have if he were going on an interview. He was asked dozens of questions to see how he presented himself. All was going well until Jared was asked the question, "Why did you leave your last job?" At this point Jared's body language shifted to indicate his sudden discomfort. He crossed his arms in a seemingly defensive stance, and tightened his facial muscles. His speech changed from casual and relaxed to tense and hesitating. It was obvious that he felt trapped by that question. (See Example 1.) The mock interviewer noticed this shift immediately, and a red flag of suspicion was raised.
What was Jared hiding?
Was he lying?
Was he fired?
Is he a dishonest individual?
Is he incompetent?
These and many other questions flashed through the minds of the real interviewers, which made Jared's acceptance for the job doubtful.

> With many qualified people for the same position, why would an employer take a chance on someone who is questionable? Why not choose someone for whom no red flags have been raised?

Dealing with Difficult Questions

Jared needed to learn how to discuss the termination of his last job openly and honestly. He also needed to do so with the reassurance that the situation had now been rectified or that because of the scheduling differences it would no longer be an issue. If he defensively went overboard with apologies, excuses, or explanations, again he would raise suspicion that there is more to this than simply a scheduling issue. (See Example 2 below.) The truth was that, for Jared, it was simply that and no more. However, until he learned how to discuss it comfortably, he was destined to repeat the scenario. Let's look at the before and after of his answer:

Example 1. Before
Mock Interviewer: "Why did you leave your last job?"

Jared: (Arms crossed, suddenly shifting in his chair) ..."Um... (looking down)...I really don't know. Guess it was downsizing."

Mock Interviewer: "Didn't they discuss it with you?"

Jared: "Well ...no ...not really."

Mock Interviewer: "Ok ...Let's go on."

After viewing the videotape in career counseling, Jared decided to try to explain....and explain...and explain...

Example 2. Before
Mock Interviewer: "Why did you leave your last job?"

Jared: "Well ...I...er ...I'm really a good worker. I worked my tail off for that company, and they know it! I've been given a really raw deal here. I worked overtime whenever I could. I had to take my kids to school in the morning and then pick them up after school. I'm a good father and they are just wonderful kids. The company knew that I needed to do this...I have joint custody of my two kids and I get them two to three days each week. My wife...well...my ex-wife used to pick them up and drop them off after her work, but then she couldn't. You see, she is a lab technician and they had to get their afternoon lab work out by 4 p.m. every day or else ...so ..."

Mock Interviewer: " I'm sorry ...we'll have to move on now."

After viewing this take, Jared realized that he was using up valuable time with irrelevant personal information. This was not helping him demonstrate why he was the perfect candidate for the job. In fact, it was revealing him as someone who wasn't sure where the boundary lies between personal information and business data. He needed to shorten his answer to fit the question.

After
Mock Interviewer: "Why did you leave your last job?"

Jared: "I was told that my work was outstanding. Because of some personal arrangements for my children, I missed out on staff meetings, which I agreed were very important to attend. I've now made other arrangements so that will no longer present any problem for me. I'm looking forward to giving this job my all!"

Mock Interviewer: (reassured) "I see. Let's move on to some other questions."

Jared began to present himself in a much more confident, comfortable manner when interviewing. He learned to look the interviewer in the eye when answering the questions and to relax enough to let his professionalism show through. Soon after, he obtained a great job and learned that his personal problems were his to work out behind the scenes— and not to share with prospective employers.

Keeping the Right Perspective

An interview is a meeting of two or more human beings. It is just as important for the interviewee to determine if there's a fit as it is for the interviewer to find the right candidate. Therefore, try to approach an interview as a learning experience that will provide necessary information in both directions. You will learn more about yourself and the world of work as you do more interviews.

You certainly want to remain true to yourself, but you also need to listen to the rules and decide if you want to play in that arena. Then, if you do go for it, give it everything you have!

Summary

Making a good impression on an interview can be the deciding factor in getting a job. The key to interviewing successfully is to be prepared. Know what characteristics your prospective employer is looking for in job candidates. Respond to interview questions in a positive way that emphasizes your skills and qualifications to do the job well. Maintain a positive disposition and dress in a professional manner. Follow up the interview with a note of thanks for the opportunity to meet.

PEOPLE WHO LOVE THEIR WORK

Name: Jeremy D. Poshkus

Hometown: Auburn, MA

Job Title: Licensed Funeral Director and Embalmer

Basic tasks of the job: Assist families during their funeral experience: Meet with family to plan and arrange the funeral and visitation, select the type of services and goods, arrange for flowers, usher guests, coordinate clergy. As an embalmer, tasks include transferring deceased from place of death, technical preparation of the body, hair, face, etc. As Director, there are management tasks, such as accounting and bookkeeping.

Why I enjoy my work: I get a lot of satisfaction from helping people during what is perhaps the most difficult time in their lives, and in making the experience as positive as possible. As an adult with Attention Deficit Disorder, I find the many different components of my profession and the constantly changing pace make this a particularly good job match for me. It's not easy, and is often emotionally draining, but there is nothing that I would rather do.

Advice to those thinking about this type of work: It is often difficult to find an entry-level position. Be patient and don't let a little rejection get you down. I went on three job interviews before getting this job. You need a minimum of an A.S. in Mortuary Science and a 2-year internship/apprenticeship. There are also exams to pass. Most Mortuary Science schools have placement assistance and access to potential employers. If you are looking for a rewarding and fulfilling career and you are a warm, caring and service/details-oriented person, this could be a career for you.

Chapter 18

LAWS AFFECTING THE JOB APPLICATION AND INTERVIEW PROCESS

Chapter Highlights

- There are laws that protect job candidates and employees in the workplace from being discriminated against due to age, gender, ethnicity, or disability. These laws restrict the information that employers may ask for on a job application or in an interview.
- It is important to understand these protections and to know how best to answer questions put forth during an interview in order to maximize your chances of being hired.

Spencer's Story

Spencer, 28 years old, was seriously injured in a motorcycle accident. Prior to the accident, Spencer enjoyed a fulfilling career in automotive mechanics. The accident left him with nerve damage that affected his arms and legs. In addition, Spencer experienced difficulties concentrating and performing detailed procedures. No longer able to stand for long periods of time, Spencer found barriers increasingly difficult to overcome in the workplace. He was devastated at the thought of not being able to work in his field.

Through rehabilitative counseling, Spencer learned enough about himself to believe that he would make an excellent mechanic supervisor. He learned which strategies would assist him in his new career, and he was prepared to stress these in an interview. He feared that prospective employers would notice his somewhat shaky gait and shy away from giving him a chance. Spencer needed to become knowledgeable in related laws that would protect his right to prove that he was the best person for the job.

The following examples are typical questions that job seekers ask, along with probable answers.

1. I have a disability and worry that I'll be discriminated against in being considered for a job. Are there laws that protect me?

Yes. The Rehabilitation Act (RA) of 1973 makes it illegal to discriminate against individuals with disabilities with respect to jobs, public education, and federal benefits. The Americans with Disabilities Act (ADA) makes it illegal to discriminate against individuals with disabilities with respect to employment in the private arena or in state and local governmental jobs or benefits. Nearly all large companies/organizations are aware of these laws, but smaller establishments may not be. The laws are designed to prohibit discrimination against someone who is otherwise an appropriate candidate for the work position, education, or benefit. They were not intended to guarantee employment for someone who clearly is not capable of handling the assigned work, even with some reasonable accommodations.

2. What is a reasonable accommodation? I am deaf in one ear. Can I still obtain a position as a doctor's receptionist? Is it reasonable to ask for a device for the telephone that enhances the sound for me?

Yes, that would be considered a reasonable accommodation. As stated earlier, reasonable accommodations are those that: a) are required to ensure equal opportunity in the job application process; b) enable the individual with a disability to perform the essential features of a job; and c) enable individuals with disabilities to enjoy the same benefits and privileges as those available to individuals without disabilities. The word "reasonable" therefore takes on a relative tone, depending on the size and capacity of the workplace in question.

Thus, if an individual is deaf in one ear but is the most qualified person to do the tasks of the job, a reasonable accommodation would be for the employer to purchase a telephone device that enhances sound, provided the employer can afford to do so. This would enable the individual to carry out the tasks in an optimal way. However, if an individual with ADHD requires a private office in order to concentrate and none is available, a private office would not be a reasonable request and therefore would not be expected.

3. I always like to get everything out in the open. When should I disclose information about my disability?

If it is an obvious disability it is important to discuss it openly, giving reassurance to the prospective employer. If you require reasonable accommodations to perform the essential functions of the job, or if, in the future, you would like to be considered for promotions for which you might require accommodations, it may be necessary to disclose your disability.

If your disability is not obvious and you don't suspect that you will require any accommodations from the employer, then it may not be necessary to discuss at all. If you have identified potentially problematic areas and can modify your method of functioning without the employer's help, then you may not want to disclose the disability at all. For example, if you have an attention-deficit/hyperactivity disorder and you have problems with remembering details, you might use certain strategies that you have found helpful, but may not want to call attention. If overcoming the effects of your disability can be accomplished without indicating you have a disability, that's even better. Some people fear that being labeled less than capable could be a threatening factor that could come back to haunt them later.

Another option is to simply state your needs without declaration of a disability. An example is the case of Bess:

"I was the new employee at work and wanted to do my best. We had weekly staff meetings and all shared the responsibility for taking minutes. I am an adult with ADHD, and although I have never disclosed this to my employer before, I shuddered to think of what the minutes would look like when it was my turn to take them! I thought long and hard about telling my boss I had ADHD and probably wouldn't do a good job taking notes for everyone. I would have had to explain that I get so caught up in what's going on that I lose whole parts of the conversation that I needed to write down. I decided that instead of disclosing, I would state my needs simply. I approached my supervisor and, with a smile, stated: 'Taking notes appears to be very important to everyone in getting all the necessary details recorded. Therefore, I would like to bring my tape recorder with me into the meetings when it's my turn to take minutes. Is that ok?' There was no problem with that!"

There is no shame in disclosure. Quite the contrary. It can often make the difference between success and failure. However, since an employer does not need to know all of the chemical, neurological, psychological, or biological systems of your body, unless it impacts on your work, why would you want to disclose to a perfect stranger more than he needs or wants to know? You wouldn't think of declaring that you have diabetes or high blood pressure unless somehow this information was relevant to your job.

4. I went on a job interview and was asked how old I was, how many children I have, and what my estimated monthly income is. Do I have to give out that kind of information?

No. All of the above are considered illegal questions today. An employer no longer has the right to ask personal questions that don't apply to the work being discussed. The law states that it is illegal for an interviewer to ask you questions related to sex, age, race, religion, national origin, or marital status, or to delve into your personal life for information that is not job related.

5. If I am asked an illegal question, how should I answer it?

You might feel like saying something like, "You and I both know that's an illegal question. You can't ask that!" However, you also know such a statement would demonstrate your lack of business tact. Instead, decide to what extent the question bothers you. If you are offended, then you are well within your legal rights not to answer. However, if you are not offended and/or if you still want to be considered for the job, you might want to consider a softer approach, such as:

Interviewer: "Do you have young children?"
Job-Seeker: "You are probably wondering whether I have any responsibilities at home that would interfere with my ability to be reliable on the job. I can assure you that I don't. In fact, I received an award for perfect attendance at my last job."

In other words, try to imagine why you are being asked the question. What is the real concern? Then try to address the concern, instead of the question itself. Here's another example that refers to the question above:

Interviewer: "What would you estimate is your household monthly income?"
Job Seeker: "I understand that this job pays with commission only. If your concern is whether or not that cash flow method would work for me, I would prefer base salary plus commission or base salary plus bonus incentive. However, I have thought carefully about this and have decided that I can handle the cash flow method of straight commission as well."

By anticipating the real question, you might be able to sidestep the illegal question and still speak to the concern. Again, if you are offended by the question, it is within your legal right not to answer. You probably won't get the job, which is an alternative you must consider. Remember, too, that while large corporations have human resource departments with professionals who are constantly upgrading their knowledge of employment laws, small companies may be totally unaware of the current laws. Therefore, it might be that they are asking out of ignorance of the law and not out of rudeness.

6. What about health issues? Do I have to tell them I take medication?

No, with few exceptions (e.g., the Armed Services) the law protects you from having to discuss, in an interview, any health issues unless they would interfere with your performance on the job. In the case of the Armed Services, a good review of these regulations can be obtained from JKL Communications in their pamphlet, *The Armed Forces and ADD/LD*. This may be obtained at www.his.com/~plath3/ Occasionally, waivers may be obtained under individual circumstances and should be discussed with an appropriate attorney.

Let's take, for example, the question:

Interviewer: "How is your health?"

The wording of this question wouldn't be considered legal. It requires you to disclose any and all disabilities/health issues even if they are totally irrelevant to the job. That is not what the employer is entitled to know.

A more appropriately worded question might be:

Interviewer: "Do you have any disabilities or health issues that would interfere with your performance on this job?"

If the question is worded this way, the answer should always be "no." If you are applying for a job for which you are not capable, you have not done your homework!

If you need reasonable accommodation to do the job, then you might consider answering like this:

"No. I have no disabilities or health issues that would interfere with my performance on this job. In fact, my skills appear to be perfectly in line with all of your requirements. I work best when I can take notes, use a tape recorder to back up my notes and memory, and even take a one-minute walk break every now and then to refresh myself. I consider myself very qualified for this job."

A wonderful book that helps to answer that question and others like it is *Succeeding in the Workplace*, edited by Peter S. Latham, J.D., and Patricia H. Latham, J.D. (1994, JKL Communications, Washington, D.C.).

The question of formal disclosure of your disability in order to qualify for legal accommodations is still a matter of taste. It would depend upon the severity of the situation as well as your confidence level to handle the potential barriers behind the scenes with coping strategies.

Summary

It is important to realize that there are laws affecting the application and interview process. Knowing what they are and how they might affect you allows you to prepare yourself properly.

PEOPLE WHO LOVE THEIR WORK

Name: Barry Slotten

Hometown: San Diego, CA

Job title: Commercial Real Estate Broker

Basic tasks of the job: Identifying office, industrial and warehouse properties for businesses to lease, sublease, purchase or sell, and then representing clients in the transaction.

What I enjoy about my work: Working with a lot of different people with varying personalities, business requirements, and commercial real estate needs, and helping them fulfill their requirement in a timely manner and to their greatest benefit.

Advice for those thinking about this type of work: Be prepared to enter a very competitive industry requiring a lot of hard work uncovering potential opportunities, and then matching them with available product. However, when you are successful the resulting compensation can be very rewarding.

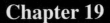

Chapter 19

GETTING OFF
ON THE RIGHT FOOT
AT YOUR NEW JOB

Chapter Highlights
- It is challenging and sometimes uncomfortable to be new on a job.
- Knowing what is expected of you can help you increase your level of comfort.
- Employers recognize the value of good interpersonal skills; it is important to work on building positive relationships with co-workers.

In a new job, you can expect to have fears and doubts. Everyone hates being the "new kid on the block." When you begin a new job, discomforts such as not knowing where the coffee pot is or where everyone goes to lunch are common. What can you do, then, to make the start-up of a new job more comfortable?

Guidelines for Starting a New Job
1. Keep a low profile.
   Try very hard not to come on too strong in the first few days of new employment. It's best to "take in" more than you "give out." Assess the social climate at your new workplace. Do people seem to chat with each other, or do they work quietly until official break time? Don't be critical about procedures or routines. Keeping opinions to yourself, initially, allows you to stay wise in your assessment of how things are run and be a respected part of "the team." Stay conservative in your dress and respect the boundaries of others until you have a chance to established yourself as a valued employee!

2. Put forth your best effort.

It is best not to ask for any special benefits early in new employment. Starting a job on Monday and asking for time off on Thursday, for an appointment, may not be the best way to make a good initial impression. Arrive promptly and leave on or after quitting time. If you must miss time at work due to an emergency, most new employers will understand, depending on the circumstances. However, repeated emergencies could reflect poorly on your performance evaluations.

3. Make an attempt to exercise your interpersonal skills.

Sometimes, when you are focusing so hard on doing a good job, you forget the social "niceties." Be aware that your employers have not only hired a worker—they have also hired a co-worker. It's common sense and nice human-to-human exchange to use social greetings (e.g., "good morning"). In general, try to maintain a pleasant demeanor throughout the work day.

4. Be careful about mistakes.

It's important to try to avoid mistakes. Initially, it might be wise to check your work more often than you normally do. Once you have established yourself as a reliable worker, occasional mistakes will be more easily tolerated.

5. It takes time.

Most experts agree that it takes six months to feel comfortable in any new position. At first you may be high on the excitement of the new job. After the first few weeks, there may be a dip in your energy because you've been trying so hard to focus on everything. Few people can keep that pace forever. If it takes six months to feel comfortable in most new positions, that is about the length of time it takes for you to be at peak efficiency. Furthermore, it takes a full year for most workers to be at a point where they are performing more than they are learning.

6. Get the support you need.

When you begin a new job, you should already have some idea of the degree of support needed for optimal job performance. Whether you choose to disclose this initially or not, you can incorporate support into your procedure. If you need to have an adaptive device on your telephone to hear better, you can obtain it. If you need a coach to help you stay focused and organized, there are ways to correspond with one via phone or e-mail. If you would benefit from a back support on your chair, you should research where to get one and the cost. Your employer may pay for this reasonable accommodation.

178

Remember that the law states that if you expect your employer to pay for a reasonable accommodation, disclosure of a disability linked to this accommodation is essential as soon as the job offer has been made. If you prefer to work from behind the scenes and secure your own adaptations, disclosure is not always necessary. Whatever the support, you should have knowledge of it, along with specific data, upon starting the job.

Summary

It is uncomfortable to be new at a job. Being prepared and understanding what is expected of you will help to offset the discomfort. Doing your best at both job tasks and interpersonal relations gets you off to a good start.

PEOPLE WHO LOVE THEIR WORK

Name: Wayne T. Laviolette, M.A. Psy.S., LLP

Hometown: South Rockwood, MI

Job title: Supervisor, Psychological Services

Basic tasks of job: Psychovocational evaluation and consultation

Why I enjoy my work: The work provides people with meaningful information to make good career decisions...especially with disabilities.

Advice for those thinking about this type of work: As you chase your career passion, always work toward developing your personal and professional level of mastery.

Chapter 20

ADJUSTING TO YOUR NEW JOB

Chapter Highlights

- Once you have a job, it is important to be aware that you may have to go through some adjustments as you learn more about your new job and become accustomed to your employer and co-workers.
- New employees go through different stages in this process of adjustment. Four stages are discussed in this chapter. Understanding what you should expect as you evolve on your new job is important.

Phil's Story

"I've moved from job to job, always looking for that 'perfect situation.' I would be 'flying high' at the start of each job, only to find out that the job wasn't perfect, and then I would crash, emotionally. For me, getting the job wasn't the hard part—it was keeping it. Career counseling has helped me to identify the things I do best and the environments that stimulate me. The research I learned to do saved me from trying out options that would have been real mistakes. Now I think I understand what went wrong in previous situations, but I'm still worried. How can I be sure that I won't crash again? How can I learn to sustain the energy and full-speed-ahead frame of mind necessary to keep plodding along? How can I evolve in my career without hopping from one place to another?"

Phil knew that he had made many career mistakes. He learned the importance of checking things out prior to leaping into a new position. His options for consideration now lined up with his total picture, which held a much better chance of success.

What Phil still needed to learn was how to evolve in his new (and hopefully improved!) situation. What happens after the good career match is identified? There are a few more steps to keep in mind.

Stages of Adjustment to Your New Job

1. The "honeymoon "stage.

   Pursuing a new job takes tremendous energy. In most cases, you will be exhilarated by the hunt, chase, and catch. You won't be able to wait to start the job, and you will dream of how wonderful it will be. Not wanting to imagine any problems, you will dare not think of any. This honeymoon period can last anywhere from a few minutes to several months. What happens to change it? Your expectations are so high and idealistic that you may not have prepared for the possibility of issues or problems that could occur. Rather than putting your head in the sand, you can anticipate and understand that, during the honeymoon stage, things tend to get glossed over. As a new employee you are on your very best behavior. As new employers, superiors are putting their best feet forward as well, giving positive feedback to "the new kid." However, once on the job, you may find that this "new kid" place you've enjoyed gives way to the employer expecting that you can move quicker, more effectively, and without as much instruction. It is at this point that the honeymoon is over!

2. The "what have I done?" stage.

   When your idealistic expectations fail, you realize that you are going to have a real job—not a fantasy land to visit each day. This step is deflating, especially if it comes as a shock to you. It is important to realize that there are no perfect jobs—all of them have positives and negatives. Remember that if you have followed the steps in this book, your chosen career is one that works for you. You can have as much certainty about that as anyone.

3. The "who can I be close to?" stage.

   One of the secrets to enjoying a career is enjoying the many friendships that come along with it. You will like some people more than others. It will take some time to get to know others and to establish friendships that are professional and comfortable. Be patient and try not to force this. Remember that it takes months to feel really comfortable on a new job.

4. The balancing stage.

Once you have been in your job for more than six months, you will want to begin to protect yourself against burnout by evaluating your life. You've learned that in order to keep things fresh and alive, you must have balance. You must continue to learn, work, and play. You must continue to challenge yourself at all three points of balance. If you continuously check that point of balance, you can be sure that you will offset burnout, lack of challenge, and boredom. This might be a good time to start a new home project, join a new group, take up a new hobby, try out for a community play, or pursue any number of other possibilities that come from your "someday I'd love to" list.

Remember that life is a process and not a product. The process is constantly changing. You will be in constant change. Therefore, with each turn of events, you will need to reassess the big picture and determine what is necessary to keep you balanced. This state of balance is essential for a rewarding, fulfilling life. It's your choice, but it's one that's well worth the time and effort.

> With so many hours of life
> spent in your career,
> you will want to follow
> the steps outlined in this book
> to find a career that
> not only supplies you with income
> but also
> *works*
> for you!

Summary

Getting a job is not the end of the career development process. There are various stages new workers go through. These stages are a part of the natural evolutionary process all workers experience. As a new employee you may experience periods where your mood fluctuates based upon your work experiences and your work expectations. Understanding that this is a common occurrence will help you be prepared as you evolve in your job. Strive for a balanced life that includes hobbies and interests, as well as the career that works for you.

APPENDIX A

SAMPLE RESUMES

Chronological Resume Style

George Washington
42901 President Avenue
Pittsburgh, PA 23505
(555) 555-0202
GW@comp.com

Objective: **Position as Sales Representative in convention bookings**

Work History

1997-2000   Cherrytree Productions, Washington DC
Sales & Marketing. Responsibilities included
generating sales of convention bookings, with
sales objectives exceeded each year, for 3 years.
Outreach to major companies required travel, presentation,
and interpersonal skills.

1990-1997   Marquis Hotel, New York, NY
Convention Planner. Successfully booked,
planned, and implemented desired format for
hotel conventions. Duties included being responsible
for details associated with mid- to large-size groups of
up to 5,000 participants.

1989-1990   Honesty Sales Associates, New York, NY
Sales Associate. Called on key corporate accounts to
present advantages of video screening products. Was
able to increase sales within a year, by over 54%.

Education and Training

1990   BA, Pittsburgh University, Pittsburgh, PA
1989   Completed sales training program, Honesty Sales Assoc.
1988   AA, Pittsburgh Community College, Pittsburgh, PA

References furnished upon request

Functional Resume Style

John D. Rockwell
34561 Oak Street
Omaha, Nebraska 70541
(555) 555-2367
JDR@loa.com

Objective: **Position as Graphic Artist**

Highlights of qualifications
- Working knowledge of paste-up, alignment and design
- Successfully designed logos for community library consortium
- Worked with creative team to implement client's ideas
- Skilled at operating reproduction camera
- Excellent proofreading abilities
- Coordinated production of mass mailings in timely fashion

Relevant Background
Graphic Design
   Established reputation as creative, organized graphic artist, utilizing strong spatial aptitude

   Wrote copy to accompany graphic designs in training manuals

   Prepared presentation packets for major corporations

   Strong sense of balance, color, form and eye appeal

Product Design
   Designed brochures, manuals and marketing packets for satisfied customers

   Developed private line of t-shirts, canvas bags and other promotional items

References furnished upon request

Combination Resume Style

Jane Tarzan
42 Swingtree Lane
Forestwoods, CA 92123
(555) 555-2309

Objective: **Entry level position in property management**

Highlights of Qualifications
- Known as "self-starter"
- Trustworthy, dependable and conscientious
- Willing to learn from the ground floor up
- Able to catch on to new things quickly

Skills and Abilities
Organizational: Demonstrated good organization in all schoolwork, projects and assignments

Interpersonal: Received excellent feedback from all teachers, summer work employers and co-workers

Outgoing: Sold more fund-raising tickets than anyone for 4 consecutive years at high school

Work History
1999-Present   JKL Nursery. Forestwoods, CA
Tree sales. Summer position while student.

1998-1999   Jungle Pet Shop, Forestwoods, CA
Assistant sales associate. Summer position.

1996-1998   Self employed child-care worker. Baby-sitting jobs.

Education
2000   Tigerwoods University, Forestwoods, CA
BA-Business

References furnished upon request

REFERENCES
AND RESOURCES

References and Resources

Bolles, R. N. (1981). *The three boxes of life*. Berkeley, CA: Ten Speed Press.

Bolles, R. N. (1999). *What color is your parachute?* Berkley, CA: Ten Speed Press.

Bramer, J. S. (1996). *Succeeding in college with attention deficit disorders*. Plantation, FL: Specialty Press, Inc.

Bramer, J.S., & Fellman, W. (1997). *Success in college and career with attention deficit disorder*. Plantation, FL: Specialty Press, Inc. (Video).

Careers for the '90s and beyond. (1994). Piscataway, NJ. Research & Education Association.

Covey, S. R. (1989). *The 7 habits of highly effective people*. New York, NY: Simon & Schuster.

Dictionary of Occupational Titles. Washington, DC: U.S. Department of Labor, Employment and Training Administration, U.S. Employment Service, 1993.

Fellman, W. (1997). *The other me: Poetic thoughts on ADD for adults, kids, and parents*. Plantation, FL: Specialty Press, Inc.

Goodman, J., & Hoppin, J. M. (1995). *Opening doors*. Rochester, MI: Continuum Center, Oakland University.

Isaacson, L. E. (1977). *Career information in counseling and teaching (3rd ed.)*. Boston, MA: Allyn and Bacon, Inc.

Knowdell, R. L., Branstead, E., & Moravec, M. (1996). *From downsizing to recovery: strategic transition options fororganizations and individuals*. Palo Alto, CA: CPP Books.

Latham, P. S., & Latham, P. H. (1994). *Succeeding in the workplace*. Washington, DC: JKL Communications.

Nadeau, K. G. (1997). *ADD in the workplace*. Bristol, PA: Brunner/Mazel, Inc.

Nadeau, K. G. (1996). *Adventures in fast forward*. New York, NY: Brunner/Mazel, Inc.

Occupational Outlook Handbook. (1999-2000 Ed.) Washington, DC: U.S. Department of Labor, Bureau of Labor Statistics.

Parker, Y. (1988). *The resume catalog: 200 damn good examples*. Berkley, CA: Ten Speed Press.

Rifkin, J. (1995). *The end of work*. New York, NY: G. P. Putnam & Sons.

Solden, S. (1995). *Women with attention deficit disorder*. Grass Valley, CA: Underwood Books.

Weddle, P. D. (1994) *Electronic resumes for the new job market*. Manassas Park, VA: Impact Publications, 1994.

Weiss, L. (1996). *A.D.D. on the job*. Dallas, TX: Taylor Publishing Co.

Zunker, Vernon G. (1994). *Using assessment results for career development. (4th ed.)*. Pacific Grove, CA: Brooks/Cole Publishing Company.

Government Agencies and Non-Profit Organizations

Attention Deficit Disorder Association (ADDA)

1788 Second St., Suite 200 • Highland Park, IL 60035
847-432-2332 • www.add.org

Children and Adults with Attention Deficit/Hyperactivity Disorder (CHADD)

8181 Professional Place • Landover, MD 20785
800-233-4050 • www.chadd.org

Clearinghouse on Disability Information

Department of Education, OSERS
Switzer Building #3132 • Washington, DC 20202
(202) 732-1241

Equal Employment Opportunity Commission

1400 L Street NW, Suite 200 • Washington, DC 20005
For ADA documents—800-669-3362
For ADA questions—800-669-4000

Interagency Committee on Employment of People with Disabilities

1400 L Street NW, Suite 200 • Washington, DC 20005
(202) 663-4568

Job Accommodation Network
PO Box 6080 • Morgantown, WV 26506
800-526-7234 • www.jan.wvu.edu

Learning Disability Association of America
4156 Library Road • Pittsburgh, PA 15234
(412) 341-1515

National Council on Disability
800 Independence Ave. SW, #814 • Washington, DC 20591
(202) 267-3232

National Rehabilitation Association (NRA)
633 S. Washington St. • Alexandra, Virginia 22314-4109
703-836-0850 • www.nationalrehab.org

Southeast Disability and Business Technical Assistance Center (SEDBTAC)
490 10th St. • Atlanta, GA 30318
800-949-4232 • www.sedbtac.org

United States Department of Justice
ADA Information Line
800-514-0301

Internet Resources for Career Seekers

There are dozens upon dozens of internet sites related to career development and the job search. We have included a sampling of such sites below:

- Career Resource Center   www.careers.org
- Minorities Job Bank   www. minorities-jb.com/
- Monster.com   www.occ.com
- Peterson's   www.petersons.com/career/
- Wall Street Journal Interactive Edition   www.careers.wsj.com
- National Association of Colleges   www.jobweb.org
  and Employers

Index